LEARN EMBOSSED CROCHET™

Branches
Cowl,
page 20

Table of Contents

CW00821637

Leaves Hat

Skill Level

■■■□ INTERMEDIATE

Finished Size

Adult woman

Finished Measurements

19 inches in circumference x 10½ inches long

Materials

- Medium (worsted) weight wool yarn:
    7 oz/440 yds/200g red
- Size H/8/5mm crochet hook or size needed to obtain gauge
- Tapestry needle
- 1½-inch decorative button

4
MEDIUM

Gauge

7 sts = 2 inches; 6 rows = 2 inches

Take time to check gauge.

Gauge Swatch

Row 1: Ch 10, dc in 4th ch from hook and in each rem ch across, turn. *(7 dc)*

Row 2: Ch 3 *(does not count as first dc)*, fpdc around each st across, turn.

Row 3: Ch 3, bpdc around each st across, turn.

Rows 4 & 5: Rep rows 2 and 3.

Pattern Notes

Weave in loose ends as work progresses.

Join with slip stitch as indicated unless otherwise stated.

Chain-3 at beginning of round worked in double crochet counts as first double crochet unless otherwise stated.

Chain-3 at beginning of round worked in back post and front post double crochet counts as first back post double crochet unless otherwise stated.

Special Stitches

V-stitch (V-st): (Dc, ch 1, dc) in indicated st.

Back post double crochet dec (bpdc dec): *Yo, insert hook from back to front to back around post of next dc, yo, pull up lp, yo, draw through 2 lps on hook, rep from * once, yo and draw through all 3 lps on hook.

Front post double crochet dec (fpdc dec): *Yo, insert hook from front to back to front around post of next dc, yo, pull up lp, yo, draw through 2 lps on hook, rep from * once, yo and draw through all 3 lps on hook.

Hat

Rnd 1 (RS): Ch 3, **join** *(see Pattern Notes)* in first ch to form ring, **ch 3** *(see Pattern Notes)*, 15 dc in ring, join in 3rd ch of beg ch-3. *(16 dc)*

Rnd 2: Ch 3 *(see Pattern Notes)*, 2 **bpdc** *(see Stitch Guide)* around same beg ch as joining, *fpdc around next dc, 3 bpdc around next dc, (fpdc, ch 1, fpdc) in next dc**, 3 bpdc around next dc, rep from * around, ending last rep at **, join in 3rd ch of beg ch-3. *(24 bpdc, 12 fpdc)*

Rnd 3: Ch 3 *(see Pattern Notes)*, bpdc around each of next 2 bpdc, *fpdc around next fpdc, bpdc around each of next 3 bpdc, fpdc around next fpdc, **V-st** *(see Special Stitches)* in next ch-1 sp, fpdc around next fpdc**, bpdc around each of next 3 bpdc, rep from * around, ending last rep at **, join in 3rd ch of beg ch-3. *(4 V-sts, 24 bpdc, 12 fpdc)*

Rnd 4: Ch 3, bpdc around same beg ch as joining, *bpdc around next bpdc, 2 bpdc around next bpdc, fpdc around fpdc, 2 bpdc around next bpdc, bpdc around next bpdc, 2 bpdc around next bpdc, fpdc around each of next 2 sts, V-st in next ch-1 sp, fpdc around each of next 2 sts**, 2 bpdc around next bpdc, rep from * around, ending last rep at **, join in 3rd ch of beg ch-3. *(4 V-sts, 40 bpdc, 20 fpdc)*

Rnd 5: Ch 3, bpdc around each of next 4 bpdc, *fpdc around next fpdc, bpdc around each of next 5 bpdc, fpdc around each of next 3 sts, V-st in next ch-1 sp, fpdc around each of next 3 sts**, bpdc around each of next 5 bpdc, rep from * around, join in 3rd ch of beg ch-3. *(4 V-sts, 40 bpdc, 28 fpdc)*

Rnd 6: Ch 3, bpdc around same beg ch as joining, *bpdc around each of next 3 bpdc, 2 bpdc around next bpdc, fpdc around next fpdc, 2 bpdc around next bpdc, bpdc around each of next 3 bpdc, 2 bpdc

around next bpdc, fpdc around each of next 4 sts, V-st in next ch-1 sp, fpdc around each of next 4 sts**, 2 bpdc around next bpdc, rep from * around, ending last rep at **, join in 3rd ch of beg ch-3. *(4 V-sts, 56 bpdc, 36 fpdc)*

Rnd 7: Ch 3, bpdc around each of next 6 bpdc, *fpdc around next fpdc, bpdc around each of next 7 bpdc, fpdc around each of next 5 sts, V-st in next ch-1 sp, fpdc around each of next 5 sts**, bpdc around each of next 7 bpdc, rep from * around, ending last rep at **, join in 3rd ch of beg ch-3. *(4 V-sts, 56 bpdc, 44 fpdc)*

Rnd 8: Ch 3, bpdc around same beg ch as joining, *bpdc around each of next 5 bpdc, 2 bpdc around next bpdc, fpdc around next fpdc, 2 bpdc around next bpdc, bpdc around each of next 5 bpdc, 2 bpdc around next bpdc, fpdc around each of next 6 sts, V-st in next ch-1 sp, fpdc around each of next 6 sts**, 2 bpdc around next bpdc, rep from * around, ending last rep at **, join in 3rd ch of beg ch-3. *(4 V-sts, 72 bpdc, 52 fpdc)*

Rnd 9: Ch 3, bpdc around each of next 8 bpdc, *fpdc around next fpdc, bpdc around each of next 9 bpdc, fpdc around each of next 7 fpdc, V-st in next ch-1 sp, fpdc around next 7 fpdc**, bpdc around each of next 9 bpdc, rep from * around, ending last rep at **, join in 3rd ch of beg ch-3. *(4 V-sts, 72 bpdc, 60 fpdc)*

Rnd 10: Sl st around next bpdc, ch 3, *bpdc around each of next 5 bpdc, **bpdc dec** *(see Special Stitches)* around next 2 bpdc, (fpdc, ch 1, fpdc) around next fpdc, bpdc dec around next 2 bpdc, bpdc around each of next 5 bpdc, bpdc dec around next 2 bpdc, **fpdc dec** *(see Special Stitches)* around next 2 fpdc, fpdc around each of next 4 fpdc, [fpdc dec around next 2 fpdc] twice, fpdc around each of next 4 fpdc, fpdc dec around next 2 fpdc**, bpdc dec around next 2 bpdc, rep from * around, ending last rep at **, join in 3rd ch of beg ch-3. *(56 bpdc, 56 fpdc, 4 ch-1 sps)*

Rnd 11: Ch 3, bpdc around each of next 6 bpdc, *fpdc around next fpdc, V-st in next ch-1 sp, fpdc around next fpdc, bpdc around each of next 7 bpdc, fpdc dec around next 2 fpdc, fpdc around each of

next 2 fpdc, [fpdc dec around next 2 fpdc] twice, fpdc around each of next 2 fpdc, fpdc dec around next 2 fpdc**, bpdc around each of next 7 bpdc, rep from * around, ending last rep at **, join in 3rd ch of beg ch-3. *(4 V-sts, 56 bpdc, 40 fpdc)*

Rnd 12: Sl st in next bpdc, ch 3, *bpdc around each of next 3 bpdc, bpdc dec around next 2 bpdc, fpdc around each of next 2 sts, V-st in next ch-1 sp, fpdc around each of next 2 sts, bpdc dec around next 2 bpdc, bpdc around each of next 3 bpdc, bpdc dec around next 2 bpdc, [fpdc dec around next 2 fpdc] four times**, bpdc dec around next 2 bpdc, rep from * around, ending last rep at **, join in 3rd ch of beg ch-3. *(4 V-sts, 40 bpdc, 32 fpdc)*

Rnd 13: Ch 3, bpdc around each of next 4 bpdc, *fpdc around each of next 3 sts, V-st in next ch-1 sp, fpdc around each of next 3 sts, bpdc around each of next 5 bpdc, [fpdc dec around next 2 fpdc] twice**, bpdc around each of next 5 bpdc, rep from * around, ending last rep at **, join in 3rd ch of beg ch-3. *(4 V-sts, 40 bpdc, 32 fpdc)*

Rnd 14: Ch 3, bpdc around same beg ch as joining, *bpdc around each of next 3 bpdc, 2 bpdc around next bpdc, fpdc around each of next 4 sts, V-st in next ch-1 sp, fpdc around each of next 4 sts, 2 bpdc around next bpdc, bpdc around each of next 3 bpdc, 2 bpdc around next bpdc, fpdc dec around next 2 fpdc**, 2 bpdc around next bpdc, rep from * around, ending last rep at **, join in 3rd ch of beg ch-3. *(4 V-sts, 56 bpdc, 36 fpdc)*

Rnd 15: Ch 3, bpdc around each of next 6 bpdc, *fpdc around each of next 5 sts, V-st in next ch-1 sp, fpdc around each of next 5 sts, bpdc around each of next 7 bpdc, fpdc around next st**, bpdc around next 7 sts, rep from * around, ending last rep at **, join in 3rd ch of beg ch-3. *(4 V-sts, 56 bpdc, 44 fpdc)*

Rnd 16: Ch 3, bpdc around same beg ch-3 as joining, *bpdc around each of next 5 bpdc, 2 bpdc around next bpdc, fpdc around each of next 6 sts, V-st in next ch-1 sp, fpdc around each of next 6 sts, 2 bpdc around next bpdc, bpdc around each of next 5 bpdc, 2 bpdc around next bpdc, fpdc around next fpdc**, 2 bpdc around next bpdc, rep from * around, ending last rep at **, join in 3rd ch of beg ch-3. *(4 V-sts, 72 bpdc, 52 fpdc)*

Rnd 17: Ch 3, bpdc around each of next 8 bpdc, *fpdc around each of next 7 sts, V-st in next ch-1 sp, fpdc around each of next 7 sts, bpdc around each of next 9 bpdc, fpdc around next st**, bpdc around each of next 9 sts, rep from * around, ending last rep at **, join in 3rd ch of beg ch-3. *(4 V-sts, 72 bpdc, 60 fpdc)*

Rnd 18: Sl st in next bpdc, ch 3, *bpdc around each of next 5 bpdc, bpdc dec around next 2 bpdc, fpdc dec around next 2 fpdc, fpdc around each of next 4 sts, [fpdc dec around next 2 fpdc] twice, fpdc around each of next 4 sts, fpdc dec around next 2 fpdc, bpdc dec around next 2 bpdc, bpdc around next 5 bpdc, bpdc dec around next 2 bpdc, (fpdc, ch 1, fpdc) in next fpdc**, bpdc dec around next 2 bpdc, rep from * around, ending last rep at **, join in 3rd ch of beg ch-3. *(56 bpdc, 56 fpdc)*

Rnd 19: Ch 3, bpdc around each of next 6 bpdc, *fpdc dec around next 2 sts, fpdc around each of next 2 sts, [fpdc dec around next 2 sts] twice, fpdc around each of next 2 fpdc, fpdc dec around next 2 sts, bpdc around each of next 7 bpdc, fpdc around next fpdc, V-st in next ch-1 sp, fpdc around next fpdc**, bpdc around each of next 7 bpdc, rep from * around, ending last rep at **, join in 3rd ch of beg ch-3. *(4 V-sts, 56 bpdc, 40 fpdc)*

Rnd 20: Sl st in next bpdc, ch 3, *bpdc around each of next 3 bpdc, bpdc dec around next 2 bpdc, [fpdc dec around next 2 sts] 4 times, bpdc dec around next 2 bpdc, bpdc around each of next 3 bpdc, bpdc dec around next 2 bpdc, fpdc around each of next 2 sts, V-st in next ch-1 sp, fpdc around each of next 2 sts**, bpdc dec around next 2 bpdc, rep from * around, ending last rep at **, join in 3rd ch of beg ch-3. *(4 V-sts, 40 bpdc, 32 fpdc)*

Rnd 21: Ch 3, bpdc around each of next 4 bpdc, *[fpdc dec around next 2 sts] twice, bpdc around each of next 5 bpdc, fpdc around each of next 3 sts, V-st in next ch-1 sp, fpdc around each of next 3 sts**, bpdc around next 5 bpdc, rep from * around, ending last rep at **, join in 3rd ch of beg ch-3. *(4 V-sts, 40 bpdc, 32 fpdc)*

Rnd 22: Ch 3, bpdc around same beg ch as joining, *bpdc around each of next 3 bpdc, 2 bpdc around next bpdc, fpdc dec around next 2 sts, 2 bpdc around next bpdc, bpdc around each of next 3 bpdc, 2 bpdc around next bpdc, fpdc around each of next 4 sts, V-st in next ch-1 sp, fpdc around each of next 4 sts**, 2 bpdc around next bpdc, rep from * around, ending last rep at **, join in 3rd ch of beg ch-3. *(4 V-sts, 56 bpdc, 36 fpdc)*

Rnd 23: Ch 3, bpdc around each of next 6 bpdc, *fpdc around next st, bpdc around each of next 7 bpdc, fpdc around each of next 5 sts, V-st in next ch-1 sp, fpdc around each of next 5 sts**, bpdc around each of next 7 bpdc, rep from * around, ending last rep at **, join in 3rd ch of beg ch-3. *(4 V-sts, 56 bpdc, 44 fpdc)*

Rnd 24: Sl st in next bpdc, ch 3, *bpdc around each of next 3 bpdc, bpdc dec around next 2 bpdc, fpdc around next fpdc, bpdc dec around next 2 bpdc, bpdc around each of next 3 bpdc, bpdc dec around next 2 bpdc, fpdc around each of next 6 sts, V-st in next ch-1 sp, fpdc around each of next 6 sts**, bpdc dec around next 2 bpdc, rep from * around, ending last rep at **, join in 3rd ch of beg ch-3. *(4 V-sts, 40 bpdc, 52 fpdc)*

Rnd 25: Ch 3, bpdc around each of next 4 bpdc, *fpdc around next fpdc, bpdc around each of next 5 bpdc, fpdc around each of next 7 sts, V-st in next ch-1 sp, fpdc around each of next 7 sts**, bpdc around each of next 5 bpdc, rep from * around, ending last rep at **, join in 3rd ch of beg ch-3. *(4 V-sts, 40 bpdc, 60 fpdc)*

Rnd 26: Sl st in next bpdc, ch 3, *bpdc around next bpdc, bpdc dec around next 2 bpdc, fpdc around next fpdc, bpdc dec around next 2 bpdc, bpdc around next bpdc, bpdc dec around next 2 bpdc, fpdc dec around next 2 sts, fpdc around each of next 4 sts, [fpdc dec around next 2 sts] twice, fpdc around each of next 4 sts, fpdc dec around next 2 sts**, bpdc dec around next 2 bpdc, rep from * around, ending last rep at **, join in 3rd ch of beg ch-3. *(24 bpdc, 52 fpdc)*

Rnd 27: Ch 3, bpdc around each of next 2 sts, *fpdc around next fpdc, bpdc around each of next 3 sts, fpdc dec around next 2 sts, fpdc around each of next 8 sts, fpdc dec around next 2 sts**, bpdc around each of next 3 sts, rep from * around, ending last rep at **, join in 3rd ch of beg ch-3. *(24 bpdc, 44 fpdc)*

Rnd 28: Ch 3 *(does not count as a st)*, dc in first st and in each st around, join in 3rd ch of beg ch-3. *(68 dc)*

Rnds 29–31: Ch 3, fpdc around next st, [bpdc around next st, fpdc around next st] around, join in 3rd ch of beg ch-3. At end of last rnd, fasten off.

Finishing
Referring to photo for placement, sew button to Hat. ●

Leaves Purse

Skill Level

 INTERMEDIATE

Finished Measurements

16 inches wide x 16 inches deep, excluding Handles

Materials

- Medium (worsted) weight acrylic yarn:
  21 oz/1,536 yds/600g red
- Size H/8/5mm crochet hook or size needed to obtain gauge
- Tapestry needle
- Sewing needle
- Matching sewing thread
- ⅜-inch-diameter natural cotton rope braid: 60-inch length

Note: *This type of rope is available at major fabric stores or use comparable rope found in home improvement stores, such as nylon rope.*

Gauge

7 sts = 2 inches; 5 rows = 2 inches

Take time to check gauge.

Gauge Swatch

Row 1: Ch 10, dc in 4th ch from hook and in each rem ch across, turn. *(7 dc)*

Row 2: Ch 3 *(does not count as first dc)*, fpdc around each st across, turn.

Row 3: Ch 3, bpdc around each st across, turn.

Rows 4 & 5: Rep rows 2 and 3.

Pattern Notes

Use a ⅜-inch diameter rope in Handle for a stronger and more polished look. Cotton or nylon comparable ropes are available at craft and home improvement stores. However, instructions for Handle can be followed without including rope.

Weave in loose ends as work progresses.

Join with slip stitch as indicated unless otherwise stated.

Chain-3 at beginning of round worked in double crochet counts as first double crochet unless otherwise stated.

Chain-3 at beginning of round worked in back post double crochet and front post double crochet counts as first back post double crochet unless otherwise stated.

Special Stitches

V-stitch (V-st): (Dc, ch 1, dc) in indicated st.

Back post double crochet dec (bpdc dec): *Yo, insert hook from back to front to back around post of next dc, yo, pull up lp, yo, draw through 2 lps on hook, rep from * once, yo and draw through all 3 lps on hook.

Front post double crochet dec (fpdc dec): *Yo, insert hook from front to back to front around post of next dc, yo, pull up lp, yo, draw through 2 lps on hook, rep from * once, yo and draw through all 3 lps on hook.

Purse

Motif
Make 15.

Rnd 1 (RS): Ch 4, **join** (see Pattern Notes) in first ch to form ring, ch 1, 12 sc in ring, join in first sc. (12 sc)

Rnd 2: Ch 3 (see Pattern Notes), dc in same st as beg ch-3, 2 dc in each rem sc around, join in 3rd ch of beg ch-3. (24 dc)

Rnd 3: Ch 3 (see Pattern Notes), 2 **bpdc** (see Stitch Guide) around same beg ch-3 as joining, *fpdc (see Stitch Guide) around next dc, 3 bpdc around next dc, (fpdc, ch 1, fpdc) around next dc**, 3 bpdc in next dc, rep from * around, ending last rep at **, join in 3rd ch of beg ch-3. (36 bpdc, 18 fpdc, 6 ch-1 sps)

Rnd 4: Ch 3, bpdc around each of next 2 bpdc, *fpdc around next fpdc, bpdc around each of next 3 bpdc, fpdc around next fpdc, **V-st** (see Special Stitches) in next ch-1 sp, fpdc around next fpdc**, bpdc around next 3 bpdc, rep from * around, ending last rep at **, join in 3rd ch of beg ch-3. (6 V-sts, 36 bpdc, 18 fpdc)

Rnd 5: Ch 3, bpdc around same bpdc as beg ch, *bpdc around next bpdc, 2 bpdc around next bpdc, fpdc around next fpdc, 2 bpdc around next bpdc, bpdc around next bpdc, 2 bpdc around next bpdc, fpdc around each of next 2 sts, V-st in next ch-1 sp, fpdc around each of next 2 sts**, 2 bpdc around next bpdc, rep from * around, ending last rep at **, join in 3rd ch of beg ch-3. (6 V-sts, 60 bpdc, 30 fpdc)

Rnd 6: Ch 3, bpdc around each of next 4 bpdc, *fpdc around next fpdc, bpdc around each of next 5 bpdc, fpdc around each of next 3 sts, V-st in next ch-1 sp, fpdc around each of next 3 sts**, bpdc around each of next 5 bpdc, rep from * around, ending last rep at **, join in 3rd ch of beg ch-3. (6 V-sts, 60 bpdc, 42 fpdc)

Rnd 7: Ch 3, bpdc around same beg ch-3 as joining, *bpdc around each of next 3 bpdc, 2 bpdc around next bpdc, fpdc around next fpdc, 2 bpdc around next bpdc, bpdc around each of next 3 bpdc, 2 bpdc around next bpdc, fpdc around each of next 4 sts, V-st around next ch-1 sp, fpdc around each of next 4 sts**, 2 bpdc around next bpdc, rep from * around, ending last rep at **, join in 3rd ch of beg ch-3. (6 V-sts, 84 bpdc, 54 fpdc)

Rnd 8: Ch 3, bpdc around each of next 6 bpdc, *fpdc around next fpdc, bpdc around each of next 7 bpdc, fpdc around each of next 5 sts, V-st in next ch-1 sp, fpdc around each of next 5 sts**, bpdc around each of next 7 bpdc, rep from * around, ending last rep at **, join in 3rd ch of beg ch-3. (6 V-sts, 84 bpdc, 66 fpdc)

Rnd 9: Ch 3, bpdc around same beg ch-3 as joining, *bpdc around each of next 5 bpdc, 2 bpdc around next bpdc, fpdc around next fpdc, 2 bpdc in next bpdc, bpdc around each of next 5 bpdc, 2 bpdc around next bpdc, fpdc around each of next 6 fpdc, V-st in next ch-1 sp, fpdc around each of next

6 fpdc**, 2 bpdc around next bpdc, rep from * around, ending last rep at **, join in 3rd ch of beg ch-3. *(6 V-sts, 108 bpdc, 78 fpdc)*

Rnd 10: Ch 3, bpdc around each of next 8 bpdc, *fpdc around next fpdc, bpdc around each of next 9 bpdc, fpdc around each of next 7 fpdc, V-st in next ch-1 sp, fpdc around each of next 7 fpdc**, bpdc around each of next 9 bpdc, rep from * around, ending last rep at **, join in 3rd ch of beg ch-3. *(6 V-sts, 108 bpdc, 90 fpdc)*

Rnd 11: Sl st around next bpdc, ch 3, *bpdc around each of next 5 bpdc, **bpdc dec** *(see Special Stitches)* around next 2 bpdc, (fpdc, ch 1, fpdc) around next fpdc, bpdc dec around next 2 bpdc, bpdc around each of next 5 bpdc, bpdc dec around next 2 bpdc, **fpdc dec** *(see Special Stitches)* around next 2 fpdc, fpdc around each of next 4 fpdc, [fpdc dec around next 2 fpdc] twice, fpdc around each of next 4 fpdc, fpdc dec around next 2 fpdc**, bpdc dec around next 2 bpdc, rep from * around, ending last rep at **, join in 3rd ch of beg ch-3. *(84 bpdc, 84 fpdc)*

Rnd 12: Ch 3, bpdc around each of next 6 bpdc, *fpdc around next fpdc, V-st in next ch-1 sp, fpdc around next fpdc, bpdc around each of next 7 bpdc, fpdc dec around next 2 fpdc, fpdc around each of next 2 fpdc, [fpdc dec around next 2 fpdc] twice, fpdc around each of next 2 fpdc, fpdc dec around next 2 fpdc**, bpdc around each of next 7 bpdc, rep from * around, ending last rep at **, join in 3rd ch of beg ch-3. *(6 V-sts, 84 bpdc, 60 fpdc)*

Rnd 13: Sl st around next bpdc, ch 3, *bpdc around each of next 3 bpdc, bpdc dec around next 2 bpdc, fpdc around each of next 2 sts, V-st in next ch-1 sp, fpdc around each of next 2 sts, bpdc dec around next 2 bpdc, bpdc around each of next 3 bpdc, bpdc dec around next 2 bpdc, [fpdc dec around next 2 fpdc] 4 times**, bpdc dec around next 2 bpdc, rep from * around, ending last rep at **, join in 3rd ch of beg ch-3. *(6 V-sts, 60 bpdc, 48 fpdc)*

Rnd 14: Ch 3, bpdc around each of next 4 bpdc, *fpdc around each of next 3 sts, V-st in next ch-1 sp, fpdc around each of next 3 sts, bpdc around each of next 5 bpdc, [fpdc dec around next 2 fpdc] twice**, bpdc around each of next 5 sts, rep from * around, ending last rep at **, join in 3rd ch of beg ch-3. *(6 V-sts, 60 bpdc, 48 fpdc)*

Rnd 15: Sl st around next bpdc, ch 3, *bpdc around next bpdc, bpdc dec around next 2 bpdc, fpdc around each of next 4 sts, V-st in next ch-1 sp, fpdc around each of next 4 sts, bpdc dec around next 2 bpdc, bpdc around next bpdc, bpdc dec around next 2 bpdc, fpdc dec around next 2 fpdc**, bpdc dec around next 2 bpdc, rep from * around, ending last rep at **, join in 3rd ch of beg ch-3. *(6 V-sts, 36 bpdc, 54 fpdc)*

Rnd 16: Ch 3, bpdc around each of next 2 bpdc, *fpdc around each of next 5 sts, V-st in next ch-1 sp, fpdc around each of next 5 sts, bpdc around each of next 3 bpdc, fpdc around next st**, bpdc around each of next 3 sts, rep from * around, ending last rep at **, join in 3rd ch of beg ch-3. *(6 V-sts, 36 bpdc, 66 fpdc)*

Rnd 17: Ch 3, bpdc around same beg ch-3 as joining, *bpdc around next bpdc, 2 bpdc around next bpdc, fpdc around each of next 6 sts, V-st in next ch-1 sp, fpdc around each of next 6 sts, 2 bpdc around next bpdc, bpdc around next bpdc, 2 bpdc around next bpdc, fpdc around next fpdc**, 2 bpdc around next bpdc, rep from * around, ending last rep at **, join in 3rd ch of beg ch-3. *(6 V-sts, 60 bpdc, 78 fpdc)*

Rnd 18: Ch 3, bpdc around each of next 4 bpdc, *fpdc around each of next 7 sts, V-st in next ch-1 sp, fpdc around each of next 7 sts, bpdc around each of next 5 bpdc, fpdc around next st**, bpdc around each of next 5 sts, rep from * around, ending last rep at **, join in 3rd ch of beg ch-3. *(6 V-sts, 60 bpdc, 90 fpdc)*

Rnd 19: Ch 3, bpdc around same beg ch-3 as joining, *bpdc around each of next 3 bpdc, 2 bpdc around next bpdc, fpdc dec around next 2 fpdc, fpdc around each of next 4 sts, [fpdc dec around next 2 fpdc] twice, fpdc around each of next 4 sts, fpdc dec around next 2 fpdc, 2 bpdc around next bpdc, bpdc around each of next 3 bpdc, 2 bpdc around next bpdc, (fpdc, ch 1, fpdc) in next fpdc**, 2 bpdc around next bpdc, rep from * around, ending last rep at **, join in 3rd ch of beg ch-3. *(84 bpdc, 84 fpdc, 6 ch-1 sps)*

Rnd 20: Ch 3, bpdc around each of next 6 bpdc, *fpdc dec around next 2 sts, fpdc around each of next 2 sts, [fpdc dec around next 2 sts] twice, fpdc around each of next 2 fpdc, fpdc dec around next 2 sts, bpdc around each of next 7 bpdc, fpdc around next fpdc, V-st in next ch-1 sp, fpdc around next fpdc**, bpdc around each of next 7 bpdc, rep from * around, ending last rep at **, join in 3rd ch of beg ch-3. *(6 V-sts, 84 bpdc, 60 fpdc)*

Rnd 21: Ch 3, bpdc around same beg ch-3 as joining, *bpdc around each of next 5 bpdc, 2 bpdc around next bpdc, [fpdc dec around next 2 fpdc] 4 times, 2 bpdc around next bpdc, bpdc around each of next 5 bpdc, 2 bpdc around next bpdc, fpdc around each of next 2 fpdc, V-st in next ch-1 sp, fpdc around each of next 2 fpdc**, 2 bpdc in next bpdc, rep from * around,ending last rep at **, join in 3rd ch of beg ch-3. *(6 V-sts, 108 bpdc, 48 fpdc)*

Rnd 22: Ch 3, bpdc around each of next 8 bpdc, *[fpdc dec around next 2 sts] twice, bpdc around each of next 9 bpdc, fpdc around each of next 3 sts, V-st in next ch-1 sp, fpdc around each of next 3 sts**, bpdc around each of next 9 bpdc, rep from * around, ending last rep at **, join in 3rd ch of beg ch-3. *(6 V-sts, 108 bpdc, 48 fpdc)*

Rnd 23: Sl st around next bpdc, ch 3, *bpdc around each of next 5 bpdc, bpdc dec around next 2 bpdc, fpdc dec around next 2 sts, bpdc dec around next 2 bpdc, bpdc around each of next 5 bpdc, bpdc dec around next 2 bpdc, fpdc around each of next 4 sts, V-st in next ch-1 sp, fpdc around each of next 4 sts**, bpdc dec around next 2 bpdc, rep from * around, ending last rep at **, join in 3rd ch of beg ch-3. *(6 V-sts, 84 bpdc, 54 fpdc)*

Rnd 24: Ch 3, bpdc in each of next 6 bpdc, *fpdc in next fpdc, bpdc in each of next 7 bpdc, fpdc in each of next 5 sts, V-st in next ch-1 sp, fpdc in each of next 5 sts**, bpdc in each of next 7 bpdc, rep from * around, ending last rep at **, join in 3rd ch of beg ch-3. *(6 V-sts, 84 bpdc, 66 fpdc)*

Rnd 25: Sl st around next bpdc, ch 3, *bpdc around each of next 3 bpdc, bpdc dec around next 2 bpdc, fpdc around next fpdc, bpdc dec around next 2 bpdc, bpdc around each of next 3 bpdc, bpdc dec around next 2 bpdc, fpdc around each of next 6 sts, V-st in next ch-1 sp, fpdc around each of next 6 sts**, bpdc dec around next 2 bpdc, rep from * around, ending last rep at **, join in 3rd ch of beg ch-3. *(6 V-sts, 60 bpdc, 78 fpdc)*

Rnd 26: Ch 3, bpdc around each of next 4 bpdc, *fpdc around next fpdc, bpdc around each of next 5 bpdc, fpdc around each of next 7 sts, V-st in next ch-1 sp, fpdc around each of next 7 sts**, bpdc around each of next 5 bpdc, rep from * around, ending last rep at **, join in 3rd ch of beg ch-3. *(6 V-sts, 60 bpdc, 90 fpdc)*

Rnd 27: Sl st around next bpdc, ch 3, *bpdc around next bpdc, bpdc dec around next 2 bpdc, (fpdc, ch 1, fpdc) around next fpdc, bpdc dec around next 2 bpdc, bpdc around next bpdc, bpdc dec around next 2 bpdc, fpdc dec around next 2 sts, fpdc around each of next 4 sts, [fpdc dec around next 2 sts] twice, fpdc around each of next 4 sts, fpdc dec around next 2 sts**, bpdc dec around next 2 bpdc, rep from * around, ending last rep at **, join in 3rd ch of beg ch-3. *(36 bpdc, 84 fpdc, 6 ch-1 sps)*

Rnd 28: Ch 3, bpdc around each of next 2 sts, *fpdc around next fpdc, V-st in next ch-1 sp, fpdc around next fpdc, bpdc around each of next 3 sts, fpdc dec around next 2 sts, fpdc around each of next 2 sts, [fpdc dec around next 2 sts] twice, fpdc around each of next 2 sts, fpdc dec around next 2 sts**, bpdc around each of next 3 sts, rep from * around, ending last rep at **, join in 3rd ch of beg ch-3. *(6 V-sts, 36 bpdc, 60 fpdc)*

Rnd 29: Ch 3, bpdc around same beg ch-3 as joining, *bpdc around next bpdc, 2 bpdc around next bpdc, fpdc around each of next 2 fpdc, V-st in next ch-1 sp, fpdc around each of next 2 fpdc, 2 bpdc around next bpdc, bpdc around next bpdc, 2 bpdc around next bpdc, [fpdc dec around next 2 sts] 4 times**, 2 bpdc around next bpdc, rep from * around, ending last rep at **, join in 3rd ch of beg ch-3. *(6 V-sts, 60 bpdc, 48 fpdc)*

Rnd 30: Ch 3, bpdc around each of next 4 sts, *fpdc around each of next 3 fpdc, V-st in next ch-1 sp, fpdc around each of next 3 fpdc, bpdc around each of next 5 sts, [fpdc dec around next 2 sts] twice**, bpdc around each of next 5 sts, rep from * around, ending last rep at **, join in 3rd ch of beg ch-3. *(6 V-sts, 60 bpdc, 48 fpdc)*

Rnd 31: Ch 3, bpdc around same beg ch-3 as joining, *bpdc around each of next 3 bpdc, 2 bpdc around next bpdc, fpdc around each of next 4 fpdc, V-st in next ch-1 sp, fpdc around each of next 4 fpdc, 2 bpdc around next bpdc, bpdc around each of next 3 bpdc, 2 bpdc around next bpdc, fpdc dec around next 2 sts**, 2 bpdc around next bpdc, rep from * around, ending last rep at **, join in 3rd ch of beg ch-3. *(6 V-sts, 84 bpdc, 54 fpdc)*

Rnd 32: Ch 3, bpdc around each of next 6 sts, *fpdc around each of next 5 fpdc, V-st in next ch-1 sp, fpdc around each of next 5 fpdc, bpdc around each of next 7 sts, fpdc around next st**, bpdc around each of next 7 sts, rep from * around, ending last rep at **, join in 3rd ch of beg ch-3. *(6 V-sts, 84 bpdc, 66 fpdc)*

Rnd 33: Ch 3, bpdc around same beg ch-3 as joining, *bpdc around each of next 5 bpdc, 2 bpdc around next bpdc, fpdc around each of next 6 fpdc, V-st in next ch-1 sp, fpdc around each of next 6 fpdc, 2 bpdc around next bpdc, bpdc around each of next 5 bpdc, 2 bpdc around next bpdc, fpdc around next fpdc**, 2 bpdc around next bpdc, rep from * around, ending last rep at **, join in 3rd ch of beg ch-3. *(6 V-sts, 108 bpdc, 78 fpdc)*

Rnd 34: Ch 3, bpdc around each of next 8 sts, *fpdc around each of next 7 fpdc, V-st in next ch-1 sp, fpdc around each of next 7 fpdc, bpdc around each of next 9 sts, fpdc around next st**, bpdc around each of next 9 sts, rep from * around, ending last rep at **, join in 3rd ch of beg ch-3. *(6 V-sts, 108 bpdc, 90 fpdc)*

Rnd 35: Sl st around next bpdc, ch 3, *bpdc around each of next 5 bpdc, bpdc dec around next 2 bpdc, fpdc dec around next 2 sts, fpdc around each of next 4 sts, [fpdc dec around next 2 sts] twice, fpdc around each of next 4 sts, fpdc dec around next 2 sts, bpdc dec around next 2 bpdc, bpdc around each of next 5 bpdc, bpdc dec around next 2 bpdc, (fpdc, ch 1, fpdc) in next st**, bpdc dec around next 2 bpdc, rep from * around, ending last rep at **, join in 3rd ch of beg ch-3. *(84 bpdc, 84 fpdc, 6 ch-1 sps)*

Rnd 36: Ch 3, bpdc around each of next 6 sts, *fpdc dec around next 2 sts, fpdc around each of next 2 sts, [fpdc dec around next 2 sts] twice, fpdc around each of next 2 sts, fpdc dec around next 2 sts, bpdc around each of next 7 sts, fpdc around next fpdc, V-st in next ch-1 sp, fpdc around next fpdc**, bpdc in next 7 sts, rep from * around, ending last rep at **, join in 3rd ch of beg ch-3. *(6 V-sts, 84 bpdc, 60 fpdc)*

Rnd 37: Sl st around next bpdc, ch 3, *bpdc around each of next 3 bpdc, bpdc dec around next 2 bpdc, [fpdc dec around next 2 sts] 4 times, bpdc dec around next 2 bpdc, bpdc around each of next 3 bpdc, bpdc dec around next 2 bpdc, fpdc around each of next 2 fpdc, V-st in next ch-1 sp, fpdc around each of next 2 fpdc**, bpdc dec around next 2 bpdc, rep from * around, ending last rep at **, join in 3rd ch of beg ch-3. *(6 V-sts, 60 bpdc, 48 fpdc)*

Rnd 38: Ch 3, bpdc around each of next 4 sts, *[fpdc dec around next 2 sts] twice, bpdc around each of next 5 sts, fpdc around each of next 3 fpdc, V-st in next ch-1 sp, fpdc around each of next 3 fpdc**, bpdc around each of next 5 sts, rep from * around, ending last rep at **, join in 3rd ch of beg ch-3. *(6 V-sts, 60 bpdc, 48 fpdc)*

Rnd 39: Ch 3, bpdc around same beg ch-3 as joining, *bpdc around each of next 3 bpdc, 2 bpdc around next bpdc, fpdc dec around next 2 sts, 2 bpdc around next bpdc, bpdc around each of next 3 bpdc, 2 bpdc around next bpdc, fpdc around each of next 4 fpdc, V-st in next ch-1 sp, fpdc around each of next 4 fpdc**, 2 bpdc around next bpdc, rep from * around, ending last rep at **, join in 3rd ch of beg ch-3. *(6 V-sts, 84 bpdc, 54 fpdc)*

Rnd 40: Ch 3, bpdc around each of next 6 sts, *fpdc around next fpdc, bpdc around each of next 7 sts, fpdc around each of next 5 fpdc, V-st in next ch-1 sp, fpdc around each of next 5 fpdc**, bpdc around each of next 7 sts, rep from * around, ending last rep at **, join in 3rd ch of beg ch-3. *(6 V-sts, 84 bpdc, 66 fpdc)*

Rnd 41: Ch 3, bpdc around same beg ch-3 as joining, *bpdc around each of next 5 bpdc, 2 bpdc around next bpdc, fpdc around next fpdc, 2 bpdc around next bpdc, bpdc around each of next 5 bpdc, 2 bpdc around next bpdc, fpdc around each of next 6 fpdc, V-st in next ch-1 sp, fpdc around each of next 6 fpdc**, 2 bpdc around next bpdc, rep from * around, ending last rep at **, join in 3rd ch of beg ch-3. *(6 V-sts, 108 bpdc, 78 fpdc)*

Rnd 42: Ch 3, bpdc around each of next 8 sts, *fpdc around next fpdc, bpdc around each of next 9 sts, fpdc around each of next 7 fpdc, V-st in next ch-1 sp, fpdc around each of next 7 fpdc**, bpdc around each of next 9 sts, rep from * around, ending last rep at **, join in 3rd ch of beg ch-3. *(6 V-sts, 108 bpdc, 90 fpdc)*

Note: *Following rnds are worked in continuous rnds. Do not join unless specified; mark beg of rnds.*

Rnd 43: Ch 1, sc in each st and ch-1 sp around. *(216 sc)*

Rnd 44: *Sc in each of next 6 sc, **sc dec** *(see Stitch Guide)* in next 2 sc, rep from * around. *(189 sc)*

Rnd 45: *Sc in each of next 5 sc, sc dec in next 2 sc, rep from * around. *(162 sc)*

Rnd 46: *Sc in each of next 4 sc, sc dec in next 2 sc, rep from * around. *(135 sc)*

Rnd 47: *Sc in each of next 3 sc, sc dec in next 2 sc, rep from * around, join in first sc. *(108 sc)*

Handle
Make 2.

Row 1: Ch 101, sc in 2nd ch from hook and in each rem ch across, turn. *(100 sc)*

Rows 2–8: Ch 1, sc in each sc across, turn. At end of last row, do not fasten off.

Cut a piece of rope the same length as Handle. Insert rope in middle of piece *(see Photo A)*. Hold Handle with first and last rows together and matching sts. Working through corresponding sts on both sides at same time, sl st in each st across *(see Photo B)*. Fasten off.

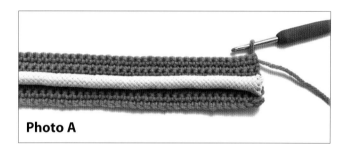

Photo A

Photo B

Large Leaf
Make 3.

Rnd 1: Ch 4, join in first ch to form ring, ch 3 *(does not count as a st)*, dc in ring, ch 1, 2 dc in ring, ch 1, dc in ring, join in first dc. *(4 dc, 2 ch-1 sps)*

Rnd 2: Ch 3 (does not count as a st), fpdc around first dc, V-st in next ch-1 sp, fpdc around each of next 2 dc, V-st in next ch-1 sp, fpdc around next fpdc, join in first fpdc. (2 V-sts, 4 fpdc)

Rnd 3: Ch 3 (does not count as a st), fpdc around first dc, fpdc around next st, V-st in next ch-1 sp, fpdc around each of next 4 sts, V-st in next ch-1 sp, fpdc around each of next 2 sts, join in first fpdc. (2 V-sts, 8 fpdc)

Rnd 4: Ch 3 (does not count as a st), fpdc around first fpdc, fpdc around each of next 2 sts, V-st in next ch-1 sp, fpdc around each of next 6 sts, V-st in next ch-1 sp, fpdc around each of next 3 sts, join in first fpdc. (2 V-sts, 12 fpdc)

Rnd 5: Ch 3 (does not count as a st), fpdc around first dc, fpdc around each of next 3 sts, V-st in next ch-1 sp, fpdc around each of next 8 sts, V-st in next ch-1 sp, fpdc around each of next 4 sts, join in first fpdc. (2 V-sts, 16 fpdc)

Rnd 6: Ch 3 (does not count as a st), fpdc around first dc, fpdc around each of next 4 sts, V-st in next ch-1 sp, fpdc around each of next 10 sts, V-st in next ch-1 sp, fpdc around each of next 5 sts, join in first fpdc. (2 V-sts, 20 fpdc)

Rnd 7: Sl st around next fpdc, ch 3 (counts as first bpdc), [fpdc dec around next 2 sts] 11 times, join in first fpdc. (11 fpdc, 1 bpdc)

Rnd 8: Sl st around next fpdc, ch 3 (counts as first bpdc), [fpdc dec around next 2 sts] 5 times, join in first fpdc. (5 fpdc, 1 bpdc)

Rnd 9: Sl st around next fpdc, ch 3 (counts as first bpdc), [fpdc dec around next 2 sts] twice, join in first bpdc. Fasten off, leaving 6-inch tail for sewing. (2 fpdc, 1 bpdc)

Small Leaf
Make 3.

Rnds 1–4: Rep rnds 1–4 of Large Leaf.

Rnd 5: Sl st around next bpdc, ch 3 (counts as first bpdc), [fpdc dec around next 2 sts] 7 times, join in first bpdc. (7 fpdc, 1 bpdc)

Rnd 6: Sl st around next fpdc, ch 3 (counts as first bpdc), [fpdc dec around next 2 sts] 3 times, join in first bpdc. (3 fpdc, 1 bpdc)

Rnd 7: Sl st around next fpdc, ch 3 (counts as first bpdc), fpdc dec around next 2 sts, join in first bpdc. Fasten off, leaving 6-inch tail for sewing. (1 fpdc, 1 bpdc)

Finishing
With tapestry needle and yarn ends, sew Large and Small Leaves to 1 Handle (see Photo C).

Photo C

Sew Handles to opposite sides of Purse. ●

Leaves Scarf

Skill Level

 INTERMEDIATE

Finished Measurements

5½ inches wide x 45 inches long

Materials

- Medium (worsted) weight acrylic yarn:
    7 oz/364 yds/200g gold
- Size I/9/5.5mm crochet hook or size needed to obtain gauge
- Tapestry needle
- 1½-inch wooden buttons: 2

Gauge

6 sc = 2 inches; 8 rows = 2 inches

Take time to check gauge.

Pattern Notes

Weave in loose ends as work progresses.

Join with slip stitch as indicated unless otherwise stated.

Special Stitches

V-stitch (V-st): (Dc, ch 1, dc) in indicated st.

Front post double crochet dec (fpdc dec): *Yo, insert hook from front to back to front around post of next dc, yo, pull up lp, yo, draw through 2 lps on hook, rep from * once, yo and draw through all 3 lps on hook.

Back post double crochet dec (bpdc dec): *Yo, insert hook from back to front to back around post of next dc, yo, pull up lp, yo, draw through 2 lps on

hook, rep from * once, yo and draw through all 3 lps on hook.

Scarf

Row 1 (WS): Ch 20, sc in 2nd ch from hook and in each of next 3 chs, dc in next ch, [sc in each of next 4 chs, dc in next ch] twice, sc in each of next 4 chs, turn. *(3 dc, 16 sc)*

Row 2 (RS): Ch 1, sc in each of first 4 sc, (**fpdc**—see Stitch Guide, ch 1, fpdc) around next st, sc in each of next 4 sc, fpdc around next st, sc in each of next 4 sc, (fpdc, ch 1, fpdc) around next st, sc in each of next 4 sc, turn. *(5 fpdc, 16 sc, 2 ch-1 sps)*

Row 3: Ch 1, sc in each of first 4 sc, **bpdc** *(see Stitch Guide)* around next st, **V-st** *(see Special Stitches)* in next ch-1 sp, bpdc around next st, sc in each of next 4 sc, bpdc around next st, sc in each of next 4 sc, bpdc around next st, V-st in next ch-1 sp, bpdc around next st, sc in each of next 4 sc, turn. *(2 V-sts, 5 bpdc, 16 sc)*

Row 4: Ch 1, sc in first 4 sc, fpdc around each of next 2 sts, V-st in next ch-1 sp, fpdc around each of next 2 sts, sc in each of next 4 sc, fpdc around next st, sc in each of next 4 sc, fpdc around each of next 2 sts, V-st in next ch-1 sp, fpdc around each of next 2 sts, sc in each of next 4 sc, turn. *(2 V-sts, 9 fpdc, 16 sc)*

Row 5: Ch 1, sc in each of first 4 sc, bpdc around each of next 3 sts, V-st in next ch-1 sp, bpdc around each of next 3 sts, sc in each of next 4 sc, bpdc around next st, sc in each of next 4 sc, bpdc around each of next 3 sts, V-st in next ch-1 sp, bpdc around each of next 3 sts, sc in each of next 4 sc, turn. *(2 V-sts, 13 bpdc, 16 sc)*

Row 6: Ch 1, sc in each of first 4 sc, [**fpdc dec** *(see Special Stitches)* around next 2 bpdc] 4 times, sc in each of next 4 sc, fpdc around next st, sc in each of next 4 sc, [fpdc dec around next 2 bpdc] 4 times, sc in each of next 4 sc, turn. *(9 fpdc, 16 sc)*

Row 7: Ch 1, sc in each of next 4 sc, [**bpdc dec** *(see Special Stitches)* around next 2 sts] twice, sc in each of next 4 sc, bpdc around next st, sc in each of next 4 sc, [bpdc dec around next 2 sts] twice, sc in each of next 4 sc, turn. *(5 bpdc, 16 sc)*

Row 8: Ch 1, sc in each of first 4 sc, fpdc dec around next 2 sts, sc in each of next 4 sc, fpdc around next st, sc in each of next 4 sc, fpdc dec around next 2 sts, sc in each of next 4 sc, turn. *(3 fpdc, 16 sc)*

Row 9: Ch 1, sc in each of first 4 sc, [bpdc around next st, sc in each of next 4 sc] 3 times, turn. *(3 bpdc, 16 sc)*

Row 10: Ch 1, sc in each of first 4 sc, fpdc around next st, sc in each of next 4 sc, (fpdc, ch 1, fpdc) around next st, sc in each of next 4 sc, fpdc around next st, sc in each of next 4 sc, turn. *(4 fpdc, 16 sc, 1 ch-1 sp)*

Row 11: Ch 1, sc in each of first 4 sc, bpdc around next st, sc in each of next 4 sc, bpdc around next st, V-st in next ch-1 sp, bpdc around next st, sc in each of next 4 sc, bpdc around next st, sc in each of next 4 sts, turn. *(1 V-st, 4 bpdc, 16 sc)*

Row 12: Ch 1, sc in each of first 4 sc, fpdc around next st, sc in each of next 4 sc, fpdc around each of next 2 sts, V-st in next ch-1 sp, fpdc around each of next 2 sts, sc in each of next 4 sc, fpdc around next st, sc in each of next 4 sc, turn. *(1 V-st, 6 fpdc, 16 sc)*

Row 13: Ch 1, sc in each of first 4 sc, bpdc around next st, sc in each of next 4 sc, bpdc around each of next 3 sts, V-st in next ch-1 sp, bpdc around each of next 3 sts, sc in each of next 4 sc, bpdc around next st, sc in each of next 4 sts, turn. *(1 V-st, 8 bpdc, 16 sc)*

Row 14: Ch 1, sc in each of first 4 sc, fpdc around next st, sc in each of next 4 sc, [fpdc dec around next 2 bpdc] 4 times, sc in each of next 4 sc, fpdc around next st, sc in each of next 4 sc, turn. *(6 fpdc, 16 sc)*

Row 15: Ch 1, sc in each of next 4 sc, bpdc around next st, sc in each of next 4 sc, [bpdc dec around next 2 sts] twice, sc in each of next 4 sc, bpdc around next st, sc in each of next 4 sts, turn. *(4 bpdc, 16 sc)*

Row 16: Ch 1, sc in each of next 4 sc, fpdc around next st, sc in each of next 4 sc, fpdc dec around next

2 sts, sc in each of next 4 sc, fpdc around next st, sc in each of next 4 sc, turn. *(3 fpdc, 16 sc)*

Row 17: Ch 1, sc in each of first 4 sc, [bpdc around next st, sc in each of next 4 sc] 3 times, turn.

Rows 18–145: [Rep rows 2–17 consecutively] 8 times or for desired length.

Edging
Rnd 1: Now working in rnd, ch 1, sc in each st and end of each row around outer edge and 3 sc in each corner, **join** *(see Pattern Notes)* in first sc. Fasten off.

Button Loops
With RS facing, holding short end at top, join yarn in 5th sc from right-hand corner, ch 8, sl st in same sc as joining, turn, work 8 sc in ch-8 sp, join in first sc. Fasten off.

Join yarn in 15th sc from same corner, ch 8, sl st in same sc as joining, turn, work 8 sc in ch-8 sp, join in first sc. Fasten off.

Finishing
Sew buttons in 5th and 15th sts of other short end or opposite button loops. ●

Leaves Blanket

Skill Level
 INTERMEDIATE

Finished Measurements
42 inches wide x 56 inches long

Materials
- Medium (worsted) weight acrylic yarn:
  52½ oz/3,435 yds/1500g blue
- Size J/10/6mm crochet hook or size needed to obtain gauge
- Tapestry needle

4 MEDIUM

Gauge
6 sts = 2 inches; 4 rows = 2 inches

Take time to check gauge.

Gauge Swatch
Row 1: Ch 9, dc in 4th ch from hook and in each rem ch across, turn. *(6 dc)*

Row 2: Ch 3 *(does not count as first dc)*, fpdc around each st across, turn.

Row 3: Ch 3, bpdc around each st across, turn.

Row 4: Rep row 2.

Pattern Notes
Weave in loose ends as work progresses.

Join with slip stitch as indicated unless otherwise stated.

Chain-3 at beginning of round worked in double crochet counts as first double crochet unless otherwise stated.

Chain-3 at beginning of round worked in back post double crochet and front post double crochet counts as first back post double crochet unless otherwise stated.

Chain-3 at beginning of rounds worked in back post double crochet and double crochet counts as first front post double crochet unless otherwise stated.

Chain-3 at beginning of round worked in front post double crochet counts as first front post double crochet unless otherwise stated.

Special Stitches
V-stitch (V-st): (Dc, ch 1, dc) in indicated st.

Back post double crochet dec (bpdc dec): *Yo, insert hook from back to front to back around post of next dc, yo, pull up lp, yo, draw through 2 lps on hook, rep from * once, yo and draw through all 3 lps on hook.

Front post double crochet dec (fpdc dec): *Yo, insert hook from front to back to front around post of next dc, yo, pull up lp, yo, draw through 2 lps on hook, rep from * once, yo and draw through all 3 lps on hook.

Blanket

Square
Make 12.

Rnd 1 (RS): Ch 4, **join** *(see Pattern Notes)* in first ch to form ring, **ch 3** *(see Pattern Notes)*, 15 dc in ring, join in 3rd ch of beg ch-3. *(16 dc)*

Rnd 2: Ch 3 *(see Pattern Notes)*, 2 **bpdc** *(see Stitch Guide)* around same beg ch-3 as joining, ***fpdc** *(see Stitch Guide)* around next dc, 3 bpdc around next dc, (fpdc, ch 1, fpdc) around next dc**, 3 bpdc around next dc, rep from * around, ending last rep at **, join in 3rd ch of beg ch-3. *(24 bpdc, 12 fpdc, 4 ch-1 sps)*

Rnd 3: Ch 3, bpdc around each of next 2 bpdc, *fpdc around next fpdc, bpdc around each of next 3 bpdc, fpdc around next fpdc, **V-st** *(see Special Stitches)* in next ch-1 sp, fpdc around next fpdc**, bpdc around each of next 3 bpdc, rep from * around, ending last

rep at **, join in 3rd ch of beg ch-3. *(4 V-sts, 24 bpdc, 12 fpdc)*

Rnd 4: Ch 3, bpdc around same beg ch-3 as joining, *bpdc around next bpdc, 2 bpdc around next bpdc, fpdc around next fpdc, 2 bpdc around next bpdc, bpdc around next bpdc, 2 bpdc around next bpdc, fpdc around each of next 2 sts, V-st in next ch-1 sp, fpdc around each of next 2 sts**, 2 bpdc around next bpdc, rep from * around, ending last rep at **, join in 3rd ch of beg ch-3. *(4 V-sts, 40 bpdc, 20 fpdc)*

Rnd 5: Ch 3, bpdc around each of next 4 bpdc, *fpdc around next fpdc, bpdc around each of next 5 bpdc, fpdc around each of next 3 sts, V-st in next ch-1 sp, fpdc around each of next 3 sts**, bpdc around each of next 5 bpdc, rep from * around, ending last rep at **, join in 3rd ch of beg ch-3. *(4 V-sts, 40 bpdc, 28 fpdc)*

Rnd 6: Ch 3, bpdc around same beg ch-3 as joining, *bpdc around each of next 3 bpdc, 2 bpdc around next bpdc, fpdc around next fpdc, 2 bpdc around next bpdc, bpdc around each of next 3 bpdc, 2 bpdc around next bpdc, fpdc around each of next 4 sts, V-st in next ch-1 sp, fpdc around each of next 4 sts**, 2 bpdc around next bpdc, rep from * around, ending last rep at **, join in 3rd ch of beg ch-3. *(4 V-sts, 56 bpdc, 36 fpdc)*

Rnd 7: Ch 3, bpdc around each of next 6 bpdc, *fpdc around next fpdc, bpdc around each of next 7 bpdc, fpdc around each of next 5 sts, V-st in next ch-1 sp, fpdc around each of next 5 sts**, bpdc around each of next 7 bpdc, rep from * around, ending last rep at **, join in 3rd ch of beg ch-3. *(4 V-sts, 56 bpdc, 44 fpdc)*

Rnd 8: Sl st in 2nd bpdc, ch 3, *bpdc around each of next 3 bpdc, **bpdc dec** *(see Special Stitches)* around next 2 bpdc, (fpdc, ch 1, 5 fpdc, ch 1, fpdc) around next fpdc, bpdc dec around next 2 bpdc, bpdc around each of next 3 bpdc, bpdc dec around next 2 bpdc, **fpdc dec** *(see Special Stitches)* around next 2 fpdc, fpdc around each of next 2 fpdc, [fpdc dec around next 2 fpdc] twice, fpdc around each of next 2 fpdc, fpdc dec around next 2 fpdc**, bpdc dec around next 2 bpdc, rep from * around, ending last

rep at **, join in 3rd ch of beg ch-3. *(40 bpdc, 60 fpdc, 8 ch-1 sps)*

Rnd 9: Ch 3, bpdc around each of next 4 bpdc, *fpdc around next fpdc, V-st in next ch-1 sp, fpdc around next fpdc, 3 bpdc around next fpdc, fpdc around next fpdc, 3 bpdc around next fpdc, fpdc around next fpdc, V-st in next ch-1 sp, fpdc around next fpdc, bpdc around each of next 5 bpdc, [fpdc dec around next 2 fpdc] 4 times**, bpdc around each of next 5 bpdc, rep from * around, ending last rep at **, join in 3rd ch of beg ch-3. *(8 V-sts, 64 bpdc, 36 fpdc)*

Rnd 10: Sl st around next bpdc, ch 3, *bpdc around next bpdc, bpdc dec around next 2 bpdc, fpdc around each of next 2 sts, V-st in next ch-1 sp, fpdc around each of next 2 sts, bpdc around each of next 3 bpdc, fpdc around next fpdc, bpdc around each of next 3 bpdc, fpdc around each of next 2 sts, V-st in next ch-1 sp, fpdc around each of next 2 sts, bpdc dec around next 2 sts, bpdc around next bpdc, bpdc dec around next 2 sts, [fpdc dec around next 2 sts] twice**, bpdc dec around next 2 bpdc, rep from * around, ending last rep at **, join in 3rd ch of beg ch-3. *(8 V-sts, 48 bpdc, 44 fpdc)*

Rnd 11: Ch 3, bpdc around each of next 2 bpdc, *fpdc around each of next 3 sts, V-st in next ch-1 sp, fpdc around each of next 3 sts, 2 bpdc around next bpdc, bpdc around next bpdc, 2 bpdc around next bpdc, fpdc around next fpdc, 2 bpdc around next bpdc, bpdc around next bpdc, 2 bpdc around next bpdc, fpdc around each of next 3 sts, V-st in next ch-1 sp, fpdc around each of next 3 sts, bpdc around each of next 3 sts, fpdc dec around next 2 sts**, bpdc around each of next 3 bpdc, rep from * around, ending last rep at **, join in 3rd ch of beg ch-3. *(8 V-sts, 64 bpdc, 56 fpdc)*

Rnd 12: Ch 3, bpdc around same beg ch-3 as joining, *bpdc around next bpdc, 2 bpdc around next bpdc, [fpdc dec around next 2 fpdc] 4 times, bpdc around each of next 5 bpdc, (fpdc, ch 1, fpdc) around next fpdc, bpdc around each of next 5 sts, [fpdc dec around next 2 fpdc] 4 times, 2 bpdc around next bpdc, bpdc around next bpdc, 2 bpdc around next bpdc, fpdc around next fpdc**, 2 bpdc around next bpdc, rep from * around, ending last rep at **, join in 3rd ch of beg ch-3. *(80 bpdc, 44 fpdc, 4 ch-1 sps)*

Rnd 13: Ch 3, bpdc around each of next 4 bpdc, *[fpdc dec around next 2 fpdc] twice, bpdc dec around next 2 bpdc, bpdc around next bpdc, bpdc dec around next 2 bpdc, fpdc around next fpdc, V-st in next ch-1 sp, fpdc around next fpdc, bpdc dec around next 2 bpdc, bpdc around next bpdc, bpdc dec around next 2 bpdc, [fpdc dec around next 2 fpdc] twice, bpdc around each of next 5 bpdc, fpdc around next fpdc**, bpdc around each of next 5 bpdc, rep from * around, ending last rep at **, join in 3rd ch of beg ch-3. *(4 V-sts, 64 bpdc, 28 fpdc)*

Rnd 14: Ch 3, bpdc around same beg ch-3 as joining, *bpdc around each of next 3 bpdc, 2 bpdc around next bpdc, fpdc dec around next 2 sts, bpdc around each of next 3 bpdc, fpdc around each of next 2 sts, V-st in next ch-1 sp, fpdc around each of next 2 sts, bpdc around each of next 3 bpdc, fpdc dec around next 2 sts, 2 bpdc around next bpdc, bpdc around each of next 3 bpdc, 2 bpdc around next bpdc, fpdc around next fpdc**, 2 bpdc around next bpdc, rep from * around, ending last rep at **, join in 3rd ch of beg ch-3. *(4 V-sts, 80 bpdc, 24 fpdc)*

Rnd 15: Ch 3, bpdc around each of next 6 bpdc, *fpdc around next fpdc, 2 bpdc around next bpdc, bpdc around next bpdc, 2 bpdc around next bpdc, fpdc around each of next 3 sts, V-st in next ch-1 sp, fpdc around each of next 3 sts, 2 bpdc around next bpdc, bpdc around next bpdc, 2 bpdc around next bpdc, fpdc around next fpdc, bpdc around each of next 7 bpdc, fpdc around next fpdc**, bpdc around each of next 7 bpdc, rep from * around, ending last rep at **, join in 3rd ch of beg ch-3. *(4 V-sts, 96 bpdc, 36 fpdc)*

Rnd 16: Ch 3 *(see Pattern Notes)*, bpdc around each of next 16 sts, 3 dc in next ch-1 sp, [bpdc around each of next 35 sts, 3 dc in next ch-1 sp] 3 times, bpdc around each of next 18 sts, join in 3rd ch of beg ch-3. *(140 bpdc, 12 dc)*

Rnd 17: Ch 3 *(see Pattern Notes)*, fpdc around each of next 17 sts, 3 fpdc around next st, [fpdc around each of next 37 sts, 3 fpdc around next st] 3 times, fpdc around each of next 19 sts, join in 3rd ch of beg ch-3. *(160 fpdc)*

Rnd 18: Ch 3, fpdc around each of next 18 sts, 3 fpdc around next st, [fpdc around each of next 39 sts, 3 fpdc around next st] 3 times, fpdc around each of next 20 sts, join in 3rd ch of beg ch-3. Fasten off. *(168 fpdc)*

Assembly

Block Squares before assembly. Referring to Assembly Diagram and with RS facing, assemble Squares in 4 rows of 3 Squares each. Sl st Squares tog. ●

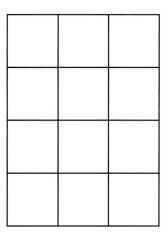

Leaves Blanket
Assembly Diagram

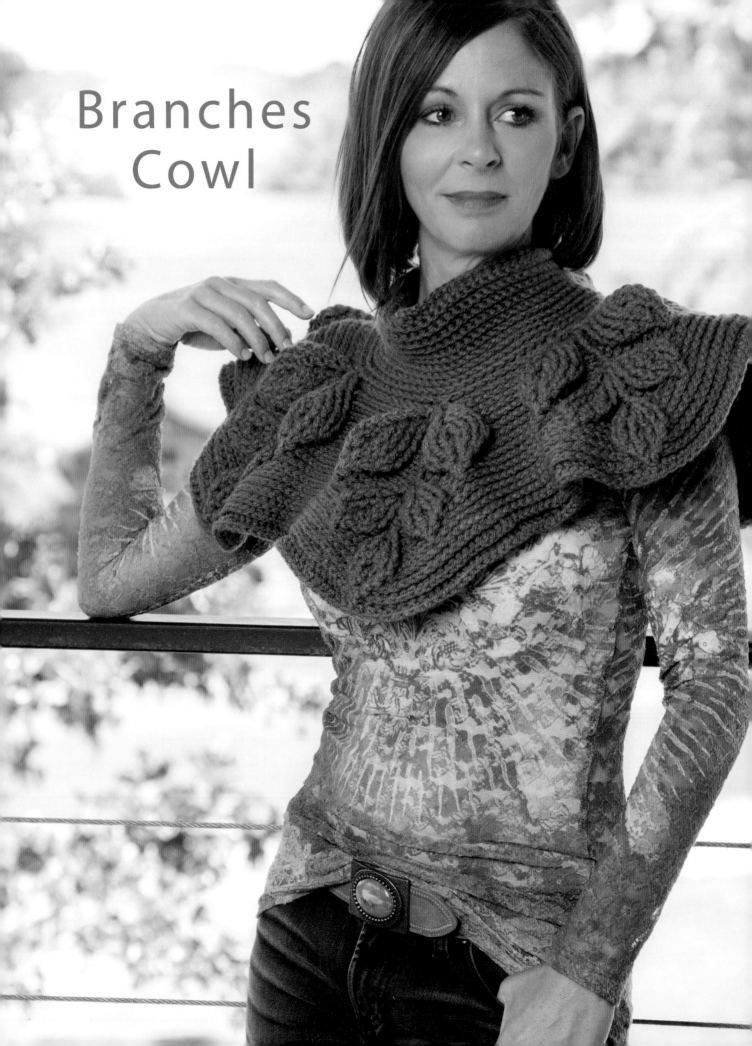

Branches
Cowl

Skill Level

 INTERMEDIATE

Finished Measurements

11 inches wide x 48 inches in circumference

Materials

- Medium (worsted) weight acrylic yarn:
    14 oz/916 yds/400g green
- Size H/8/5mm crochet hook or size needed to obtain gauge
- Tapestry needle

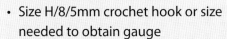

Gauge

7 sts = 2 inches; 6 rows = 2 inches

Take time to check gauge.

Gauge Swatch

Row 1: Ch 9, dc in 4th ch from hook and in each rem ch across, turn. *(6 dc)*

Row 2: Ch 3 *(does not count as first dc)*, fpdc around each st across, turn.

Row 3: Ch 3, bpdc around each st across, turn.

Rows 4 & 5: Rep rows 2 and 3.

Row 6: Rep row 2.

Pattern Notes

Weave in loose ends as work progresses.

Join with slip stitch as indicated unless otherwise stated.

Chain-3 at beginning of round worked in double crochet counts as first double crochet unless otherwise stated.

Chain-3 at beginning of round worked in front post double crochet counts as first front post double crochet unless otherwise stated.

Chain-3 at beginning of round worked in back post double crochet or front post double crochet counts as first back post double crochet unless otherwise stated.

Special Stitches

V-stitch (V-st): (Dc, ch 1, dc) in indicated st.

Front post double crochet dec (fpdc dec): *Yo, insert hook from front to back to front around post of next dc, yo, pull up lp, yo, draw through 2 lps on hook, rep from * once, yo and draw through all 3 lps on hook.

Back post double crochet dec (bpdc dec): *Yo, insert hook from back to front to back around post of next dc, yo, pull up lp, yo, draw through 2 lps on hook, rep from * once, yo and draw through all 3 lps on hook.

Cowl

Rnd 1 (RS): Ch 72, **join** *(see Pattern Notes)* in first ch to form ring, **ch 3** *(see Pattern Notes)*, dc in each ch, join in 3rd ch of beg ch-3. *(72 dc)*

Rnd 2: Ch 3 *(see Pattern Notes)*, **fpdc** *(see Stitch Guide)* around each dc, join in 3rd ch of beg ch-3.

Rnds 3–12: Rep rnd 2.

Note: *Before beg rnd 13, turn work inside out. The WS of work (with ridges) should be facing. WS now is the RS of work.*

Rnd 13 (RS): Ch 3 *(see Pattern Notes)*, *bpdc *(see Stitch Guide)* around each of next 10 sts, (fpdc, ch 1, 5 fpdc, ch 1, fpdc) around next st**, bpdc around each of next 11 sts, (fpdc, ch 1, 5 fpdc, ch 1, fpdc) around next st, rep from * around, ending last rep at **, join in 3rd ch of beg ch-3. *(66 bpdc, 42 fpdc, 12 ch-1 sps)*

Rnd 14: Ch 3, bpdc around same bpdc as beg ch-3, *bpdc around each of next 9 bpdc, 2 bpdc around next bpdc, fpdc around next fpdc, **V-st** *(see Special Stitches)* in next ch-1 sp, fpdc around next fpdc, 3 bpdc around next fpdc, fpdc around next fpdc, 3 bpdc around next fpdc, fpdc around next fpdc, V-st in next ch-1 sp, fpdc around next fpdc**, 2 bpdc around next bpdc, rep from * around, ending last rep at **, join in 3rd ch of beg ch-3. *(12 V-sts, 114 bpdc, 30 fpdc)*

Rnd 15: Ch 3, bpdc around each of next 12 bpdc, *fpdc around each of next 2 sts, V-st in next ch-1 sp, fpdc around each of next 2 sts, bpdc around each of next 3 bpdc, fpdc around next fpdc, bpdc around each of next 3 bpdc, fpdc around each of next 2 sts, V-st in next ch-1 sp, fpdc around each of next 2 sts**, bpdc around each of next 13 bpdc, rep from * around, ending last rep at **, join in 3rd ch of beg ch-3. *(12 V-sts, 114 bpdc, 54 fpdc)*

Rnd 16: Ch 3, bpdc around same st as beg ch-3, *bpdc around each of next 11 bpdc, 2 bpdc around next bpdc, fpdc around each of next 3 sts, V-st in next ch-1 sp, fpdc around each of next 3 sts, 2 bpdc around next bpdc, bpdc around next bpdc, 2 bpdc around next bpdc, fpdc around next fpdc, 2 bpdc around next bpdc, bpdc around next bpdc, 2 bpdc around next bpdc, fpdc around each of next 3 sts, V-st in next ch-1 sp, fpdc around each of next 3 sts**, 2 bpdc around next bpdc, rep from * around, ending last rep at **, join in 3rd ch of beg ch-3. *(12 V-sts, 150 bpdc, 78 fpdc)*

Rnd 17: Ch 3, bpdc around each of next 14 bpdc, *fpdc around each of next 4 sts, V-st in next ch-1 sp, fpdc around each of next 4 sts, bpdc around each of next 5 bpdc, fpdc around next fpdc, bpdc around each of next 5 bpdc, fpdc around each of next 4 sts, V-st in next ch-1 sp, fpdc around each of next 4 sts**, bpdc around each of next 15 bpdc, rep from * around, ending last rep at **, join in 3rd ch of beg ch-3. *(12 V-sts, 150 bpdc, 102 fpdc)*

Rnd 18: Ch 3, bpdc around same st as beg ch-3, *bpdc around each of next 13 bpdc, 2 bpdc around next bpdc, fpdc around each of next 5 sts, V-st in next ch-1 sp, fpdc around each of next 5 sts, 2 bpdc around next bpdc, bpdc around each of next 3 bpdc, 2 bpdc around next bpdc, fpdc around next fpdc, 2 bpdc around next bpdc, bpdc around each of next 3 bpdc, 2 bpdc around next bpdc, fpdc around each of next 5 sts, V-st in next ch-1 sp, fpdc around each of next 5 sts**, 2 bpdc around next bpdc, rep from * around, ending last rep at **, join in 3rd ch of beg ch-3. *(12 V-sts, 186 bpdc, 126 fpdc)*

Rnd 19: Ch 3, bpdc around each of next 16 bpdc, *[**fpdc dec** *(see Special Stitches)* around next 2 sts,

fpdc around each of next 2 fpdc, fpdc dec around next 2 sts] twice, bpdc around each of next 7 bpdc (fpdc, ch 1, 5 fpdc, ch 1, fpdc) around next fpdc, bpdc around each of next 7 bpdc, [fpdc dec around next 2 sts, fpdc around each of next 2 fpdc, fpdc dec around next 2 fpdc] twice**, bpdc around each of next 17 bpdc, rep from * around, ending last rep at **, join in 3rd ch of beg ch-3. *(186 bpdc, 138 fpdc, 12 ch-1 sps)*

Rnd 20: Sl st around next bpdc, ch 3, *bpdc around each of next 13 bpdc, **bpdc dec** *(see Special Stitches)* around next 2 sts, [fpdc dec around next 2 fpdc] 4 times, bpdc dec around next 2 sts, bpdc around each of next 3 bpdc, bpdc dec around next 2 sts, fpdc around next fpdc, V-st in next ch-1 sp, fpdc around next fpdc, 3 bpdc around next fpdc, fpdc around next fpdc, 3 bpdc around next fpdc, fpdc around next fpdc, V-st in next ch-1 sp, fpdc around next fpdc, bpdc dec around next 2 sts, bpdc around each of next 3 bpdc, bpdc dec around next 2 sts, [fpdc dec around next 2 sts] 4 times**, bpdc dec around next 2 sts, rep from * around, ending last rep at **, join in 3rd ch of beg ch-3. *(12 V-sts, 186 bpdc, 78 fpdc)*

Rnd 21: Ch 3, bpdc around each of next 14 bpdc, *[fpdc dec around next 2 fpdc] twice, bpdc around each of next 5 bpdc, fpdc around each of next 2 sts, V-st in next ch-1 sp, fpdc around each of next 2 sts, bpdc around each of next 3 bpdc, fpdc around next fpdc, bpdc around each of next 3 bpdc, fpdc around each of next 2 sts, V-st in next ch-1 sp, fpdc around each of next 2 sts, bpdc around each of next 5 bpdc, [fpdc dec around next 2 sts] twice**, bpdc around each of next 15 bpdc, rep from * around, ending last rep at **, join in 3rd ch of beg ch-3. *(12 V-sts, 186 bpdc, 78 fpdc)*

Rnd 22: Sl st around next bpdc, ch 3, *bpdc around each of next 11 bpdc, bpdc dec around next 2 sts, fpdc dec around next 2 sts, bpdc dec around next 2 sts, bpdc around next bpdc, bpdc dec around next 2 sts, fpdc around each of next 3 sts, V-st in next ch-1 sp, fpdc around each of next 3 sts, 2 bpdc around next bpdc, bpdc around next bpdc, 2 bpdc around next bpdc, fpdc around next fpdc, 2 bpdc around next bpdc, bpdc around next bpdc, 2 bpdc around next bpdc, fpdc around each of next 3 sts, V-st in next ch-1 sp, fpdc around each of next 3 sts, bpdc dec around next 2 sts, bpdc around next bpdc, bpdc dec around next 2 sts, fpdc dec around next 2 sts**, bpdc dec around next 2 sts, rep from * around, ending last rep at **, join in 3rd ch of beg ch-3. *(12 V-sts, 174 bpdc, 90 fpdc)*

Rnd 23: Ch 3, bpdc around each of next 16 sts, *[fpdc dec around next 2 sts] 4 times, bpdc around each of next 5 bpdc, (fpdc, ch 1, fpdc) around next fpdc, bpdc around each of next 5 bpdc, [fpdc dec around next 2 sts] 4 times, bpdc around each of next 4 sts**, bpdc around each of next 17 sts, rep from * around, ending last rep at **, join in 3rd ch of beg ch-3. *(186 bpdc, 60 fpdc, 6 ch-1 sps)*

Rnd 24: Sl st around next bpdc, ch 3, *bpdc around each of next 9 bpdc, bpdc dec around next 2 sts, bpdc around next bpdc, 2 bpdc around next bpdc, bpdc around next bpdc, 2 bpdc around next bpdc, [fpdc dec around next 2 sts] twice, 2 bpdc around next bpdc, bpdc around each of next 3 bpdc, 2 bpdc around next bpdc, fpdc around next fpdc, V-st in next ch-1 sp, fpdc around next fpdc, 2 bpdc around next bpdc, bpdc around each of next 3 bpdc, 2 bpdc around next bpdc, [fpdc dec around next 2 sts] twice, 2 bpdc around next bpdc, bpdc around next bpdc, 2 bpdc around next bpdc, bpdc around next bpdc**, bpdc dec around next 2 sts, rep from * around, ending last rep at **, join in 3rd ch of beg ch-3. *(6 V-sts, 222 bpdc, 36 fpdc)*

Rnd 25: Ch 3, bpdc around each of next 16 sts, *fpdc dec around next 2 sts, bpdc around each of next 7 bpdc, fpdc around each of next 2 sts, V-st in next ch-1 sp, fpdc around each of next 2 sts, bpdc around each of next 7 bpdc, fpdc dec around next 2 sts, bpdc around each of next 6 bpdc**, bpdc around each of next 17 sts, rep from * around, ending last rep at **, join in 3rd ch of beg ch-3. *(6 V-sts, 222 bpdc, 36 fpdc)*

Rnd 26: Sl st around next bpdc, ch 3, *bpdc around each of next 7 bpdc, bpdc dec around next 2 sts, bpdc around next bpdc, 2 bpdc around next bpdc, bpdc around each of next 3 bpdc, 2 bpdc around next bpdc, bpdc around next st, bpdc dec around next 2 sts, bpdc around each of next 3 bpdc, bpdc dec around next 2 sts, fpdc around each of next 3 sts, V-st in next ch-1 sp, fpdc around each of next 3 sts, bpdc dec around next 2 sts, bpdc around each of next 3 bpdc, bpdc dec around next 2 sts, bpdc around next st, 2 bpdc around next bpdc, bpdc around each of next 3 bpdc, 2 bpdc around next bpdc, bpdc around next bpdc**, bpdc dec around next 2 sts, rep from * around, ending last rep at **, join in 3rd ch of beg ch-3. *(6 V-sts, 222 bpdc, 36 fpdc)*

Rnd 27: Ch 3, bpdc around each of next 22 sts, [fpdc dec around next 2 sts] 4 times, bpdc around each of next 14 sts, *bpdc around each of next 23 bpdc, [fpdc dec around next 2 sts] 4 times, bpdc around each of next 14 sts, rep from * around, join in 3rd ch of beg ch-3. *(222 bpdc, 24 fpdc)*

Rnd 28: Ch 3, bpdc around same st as beg ch-3, *bpdc around each of next 7 bpdc, 2 bpdc around next bpdc, bpdc around next bpdc, 2 bpdc around next bpdc, bpdc around each of next 5 bpdc, 2 bpdc around next bpdc, bpdc around next bpdc, 2 bpdc around next bpdc, bpdc around each of next 3 bpdc, 2 bpdc around next bpdc, [fpdc dec around next 2 sts] twice, 2 bpdc around next bpdc, bpdc around each of next 3 bpdc, 2 bpdc around next bpdc, bpdc around next bpdc, 2 bpdc around next bpdc, bpdc around each of next 5 bpdc, 2 bpdc around next bpdc, bpdc around next bpdc**, 2 bpdc around next bpdc, rep from * around, ending last rep at **, join in 3rd ch of beg ch-3. *(282 bpdc, 12 fpdc)*

Rnd 29: Ch 3, bpdc around each of next 28 sts, fpdc dec around next 2 sts, bpdc around each of next 18 bpdc, *bpdc around each of next 29 bpdc, fpdc dec around next 2 sts, bpdc around each of next 18 bpdc, rep from * around, join in 3rd ch of beg ch-3. *(282 bpdc, 6 fpdc)*

Rnd 30: Ch 2 *(counts as first hdc)*, hdc in each st around, join in 2nd ch of beg ch-2. Fasten off. ●

Leaves Baby Blanket

Skill Level

■■■□ INTERMEDIATE

Finished Measurements

30½ inches wide x 37 inches long

Materials

- DK (light worsted) weight acrylic yarn:
  24½ oz/2,751 yds/700g green
- Size H/8/5mm crochet hook or size needed to obtain gauge
- Tapestry needle

Gauge

7 sts = 2 inches; 5 rows = 2 inches

Take time to check gauge.

Gauge Swatch

Row 1: Ch 10, dc in 4th ch from hook and in each rem ch across, turn. *(7 dc)*

Row 2: Ch 3 *(does not count as first dc)*, fpdc around each st across, turn.

Row 3: Ch 3, bpdc around each st across, turn.

Rows 4 & 5: Rep rows 2 and 3.

Pattern Notes

Weave in loose ends as work progresses.

Join with slip stitch as indicated unless otherwise stated.

Chain-3 at beginning of round worked in double crochet counts as first double crochet unless otherwise stated.

Chain-3 at beginning of round worked in back post double crochet and front post double crochet counts as first back post double crochet unless otherwise stated.

Special Stitches

V-stitch (V-st): (Dc, ch 1, dc) in indicated st.

Front post double crochet dec (fpdc dec): *Yo, insert hook from front to back to front around post of next dc, yo, pull up lp, yo, draw through 2 lps on hook, rep from * once, yo and draw through all 3 lps on hook.

Bobble: Holding back last lp of each st on hook, 5 dc in indicated st, yo and draw through all lps on hook.

Back post double crochet dec (bpdc dec): *Yo, insert hook from back to front to back around post of next dc, yo, pull up lp, yo, draw through 2 lps on hook, rep from * once, yo and draw through all 3 lps on hook.

Blanket

Square
Make 20.

Rnd 1 (RS): Ch 4, **join** *(see Pattern Notes)* in first ch to form ring, **ch 3** *(see Pattern Notes)*, 15 dc in ring, join in 3rd ch of beg ch-3. *(16 dc)*

Rnd 2: Ch 3 *(see Pattern Notes)*, 2 **bpdc** *(see Stitch Guide)* around same beg ch-3 as joining, ***fpdc** *(see Stitch Guide)* around next dc, 3 bpdc around next dc, (fpdc, ch 1, fpdc) around next dc**, 3 bpdc around next dc, rep from * around, ending last rep at **, join in 3rd ch of beg ch-3. *(24 bpdc, 12 fpdc, 4 ch-1 sps)*

Rnd 3: Ch 3, bpdc around each of next 2 bpdc, *fpdc around next fpdc, bpdc around each of next 3 bpdc, fpdc around next fpdc, **V-st** *(see Special Stitches)* in next ch-1 sp, fpdc around next fpdc**, bpdc around each of next 3 bpdc, rep from * around, ending last rep at **, join in 3rd ch of beg ch-3. *(4 V-sts, 24 bpdc, 12 fpdc)*

Rnd 4: Ch 3, bpdc around same beg ch as joining, *bpdc around next bpdc, 2 bpdc around next bpdc, fpdc around next fpdc, 2 bpdc around next bpdc,

bpdc around next bpdc, 2 bpdc around next bpdc, fpdc around each of next 2 sts, V-st in next ch-1 sp, fpdc around each of next 2 sts**, 2 bpdc around next bpdc, rep from * around, ending last rep at **, join in 3rd ch of beg ch-3. *(4 V-sts, 40 bpdc, 20 fpdc)*

Rnd 5: Ch 3, bpdc around each of next 4 bpdc, *fpdc around next fpdc, bpdc around each of next 5 bpdc,

fpdc around each of next 3 sts, V-st in next ch 1-sp, fpdc around each of next 3 sts**, bpdc around each of next 5 bpdc, rep from * around, ending last rep at **, join in 3rd ch of beg ch-3. *(4 V-sts, 40 bpdc, 28 fpdc)*

Rnd 6: Ch 3, bpdc around same beg ch-3 as joining, *bpdc around each of next 3 bpdc, 2 bpdc around next bpdc, 5 fpdc around next fpdc, 2 bpdc around next bpdc, bpdc around each of next 3 bpdc, 2 bpdc around next bpdc, [**fpdc dec** *(see Special Stitches)* around next 2 sts] 4 times**, 2 bpdc around next bpdc, rep from * around, ending last rep at **, join in 3rd ch of beg ch-3. *(56 bpdc, 36 fpdc)*

Rnd 7: Ch 3, bpdc around each of next 6 bpdc, ***bobble** (see Special Stitches)* in next fpdc, [3 bpdc around next fpdc, bobble around next fpdc] twice, bpdc around each of next 7 bpdc, [fpdc dec around next 2 fpdc] twice**, bpdc around each of next 7 bpdc, rep from * around, ending last rep at **, join in 3rd ch of beg ch-3. *(12 bobbles, 80 bpdc, 8 fpdc)*

Rnd 8: Sl st in 2nd bpdc, ch 3, *bpdc around each of next 3 bpdc, **bpdc dec** *(see Special Stitches)* around next 2 bpdc, dc in next st, [bpdc around each of next 3 bpdc, dc in next st] twice, bpdc dec around next 2 bpdc, bpdc around each of next 3 bpdc, bpdc dec around next 2 bpdc, fpdc dec around next 2 fpdc**, bpdc dec around next 2 bpdc, rep from * around, ending last rep at **, join in 3rd ch of beg ch-3. *(64 bpdc, 4 fpdc, 12 dc)*

Rnd 9: Ch 3, bpdc around each of next 8 sts, 3 bpdc around next st, [bpdc around each of next 19 sts, 3 bpdc around next st] 3 times, bpdc around each of next 10 sts, join in 3rd ch of beg ch-3. *(88 bpdc)*

Rnd 10: Ch 3, fpdc around next bpdc, [bpdc around next bpdc, fpdc around each of next bpdc] 4 times, (bpdc, fpdc, bpdc) around next bpdc, *fpdc around next bpdc, [bpdc around next bpdc, fpdc around next bpdc] 10 times, (bpdc, fpdc, bpdc) around next bpdc, rep from * twice, fpdc around next st, [bpdc

around next bpdc, fpdc around next bpdc] 5 times, join in 3rd ch of beg ch-3. *(48 bpdc, 48 fpdc)*

Rnd 11: Ch 3, [fpdc around next fpdc, bpdc around next bpdc] 5 times, *(fpdc, bpdc, fpdc) around next fpdc, bpdc around next bpdc, [fpdc around next fpdc, bpdc around next bpdc] 11 times, rep from * twice, (fpdc, bpdc, fpdc) around next fpdc, [bpdc around next bpdc, fpdc around next bpdc] 6 times, join in 3rd ch of beg ch-3. *(52 bpdc, 52 fpdc)*

Assembly

Block Squares before assembly. Referring to Assembly Diagram and with RS facing, assemble Squares in 5 rows of 4 Squares each. Sl st Squares tog. ●

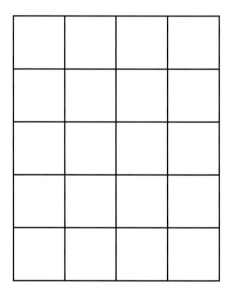

Leaves Baby Blanket
Assembly Diagram

Daisy
Vest

Skill Level

 **INTERMEDIATE**

Finished Sizes

Instructions given fit woman's size small/medium; changes for large/X-large and 2X-large/3X-large are in [ ].

Finished Measurements

Back Motif: 17½ inches *(small/medium)* [19½ inches *(large/X-large)*, 20½ inches *(2X-large/3X-large)*] in diameter

Armhole: 8 *(small/medium)* [8½ *(large/X-large)*, 8½ *(2X-large/3X-large)*] inches across

Width from side to side across back: 33 *(small/medium)* [41 *(large/X-large)*, 45 *(2X-large/3X-large)*] inches

Materials

- Medium (worsted) weight acrylic yarn:
    1,200 (size small/medium),
    1,350 (size large/X-large) and
    1,500 (size 2X-large/3X-large) yds beige
- Size H/8/5mm crochet hook or size needed to obtain gauge
- Tapestry needle

Gauge

7 sts = 2 inches; 5 rows = 2 inches

Take time to check gauge.

Gauge Swatch

Row 1: Ch 10, dc in 4th ch from hook and in each rem ch across, turn. *(7 dc)*

Row 2: Ch 3 *(does not count as a st)*, fpdc around each st across, turn.

Row 3: Ch 3, bpdc around each st across, turn.

Rows 4 & 5: Rep rows 2 and 3.

Pattern Notes

In some rounds throughout pattern, such as rounds 5 and 6, Motif may cup or ruffle. This is not an error in the pattern. Subsequent rounds will even out the cupping or ruffling and create the embossed look.

Weave in loose ends as work progresses.

Join with slip stitch as indicated unless otherwise stated.

Chain-3 at beginning of round or row worked in double crochet counts as first double crochet unless otherwise stated.

Chain-3 at beginning of round worked in double crochet or front post double crochet counts as first double crochet unless otherwise stated.

Special Stitches

V-stitch (V-st): (Dc, ch 1, dc) in indicated st.

Front post double crochet dec (fpdc dec): *Yo, insert hook from front to back to front around post of next dc, yo, pull up lp, yo, draw through 2 lps on hook, rep from * once, yo and draw through all 3 lps on hook.

Vest

Back Motif

Rnd 1 (RS): Ch 4, **join** *(see Pattern Notes)* in first ch to form ring, ch 1, 6 sc in ring, join in first sc. *(6 sc)*

Rnd 2: Ch 1, (sc, **dtr**—see Stitch Guide) in each sc around, join in first sc. *(6 dtr, 6 sc)*

Rnd 3: Ch 1, dtr in first st, (sc, dtr) in next st, sc in next sc, (dtr, sc) in next st, [dtr in next st, (sc, dtr) in next st, sc in next st, (dtr, sc) in next st] twice, join in first dtr. *(9 dtr, 9 sc)*

Rnd 4: Ch 1, sc in first dtr, dtr in next st, (sc, dtr) in next st, [sc in next st, dtr in next st, (sc, dtr) in next st] 5 times, join in first sc. *(12 dtr, 12 sc)*

Learn Embossed Crochet

Rnd 5: Ch 3 *(see Pattern Notes)*, dc in each of next 2 sts, 2 dc in next st, [dc in each of next 3 sts, 2 dc in next st] 5 times, join in 3rd ch of beg ch-3. *(30 dc)*

Rnd 6: Ch 1, **fpdc** *(see Stitch Guide)* around beg ch-3, fpdc around next dc, ch 1, fpdc around each of next 2 dc, 3 **bpdc** *(see Stitch Guide)* around next dc, *fpdc around each of next 2 dc, ch 1, fpdc around each of next 2 dc, 3 bpdc around next dc, rep from * around, join in first fpdc. *(24 fpdc, 18 bpdc, 6 ch-1 sps)*

Rnd 7: Ch 1, 2 fpdc around first fpdc, *fpdc around next fpdc, **V-st** *(see Special Stitches)* in next ch-1 sp, fpdc around next fpdc, 2 fpdc around next fpdc, bpdc around each of next 3 bpdc**, 2 fpdc around next fpdc, rep from * around, ending last rep at **, join in first fpdc. *(6 V-sts, 36 fpdc, 18 bpdc)*

Rnd 8: Ch 1, fpdc around each of first 4 fpdc, *V-st in next ch-1 sp, fpdc around each of next 4 sts, 2 bpdc around next bpdc, bpdc around next bpdc, 2 bpdc around next bpdc**, fpdc around each of next 4 sts, rep from * around, ending last rep at **, join in first fpdc. *(6 V-sts, 48 fpdc, 30 bpdc)*

Rnd 9: Ch 1, 2 fpdc around first fpdc, *fpdc around each of next 4 sts, V-st in next ch-1 sp, fpdc around each of next 4 sts, 2 fpdc around next fpdc, bpdc around each of next 5 bpdc**, 2 fpdc around next fpdc, rep from * around, ending last rep at **, join in first fpdc. *(6 V-sts, 72 fpdc, 30 bpdc)*

Rnd 10: Ch 1, fpdc around first fpdc, fpdc around each of next 6 sts, *V-st in next ch-1 sp, fpdc around each of next 7 sts, 2 bpdc around next bpdc, bpdc around each of next 3 bpdc, 2 bpdc around next bpdc**, fpdc around each of next 7 sts, rep from * around, ending last rep at **, join in first fpdc. *(6 V-sts, 84 fpdc, 42 bpdc)*

Rnd 11: Ch 1, 2 fpdc around first fpdc, *fpdc around each of next 7 sts, V-st in next ch-1 sp, fpdc around each of next 7 sts, 2 fpdc around next fpdc, bpdc around each of next 7 bpdc**, 2 fpdc around next fpdc, rep from * around, ending last rep at **, join in first fpdc. *(6 V-sts, 108 fpdc, 42 bpdc)*

Rnd 12: Ch 1, **fpdc dec** (see Special Stitches) around first 2 sts, *fpdc around each of next 6 sts, [fpdc dec around next 2 sts] twice, fpdc around each of next 6 fpdc, fpdc dec around next 2 sts, 2 bpdc around next bpdc, bpdc around each of next 5 bpdc, 2 bpdc around next bpdc**, fpdc dec around next 2 sts, rep from * around, ending last rep at **, join in first fpdc. (96 fpdc, 54 bpdc)

Rnd 13: Ch 1, fpdc dec around first 2 sts, *fpdc around each of next 4 sts, [fpdc dec around next 2 sts] twice, fpdc around each of next 4 sts, fpdc dec around next 2 sts, bpdc around each of next 9 bpdc**, fpdc dec around next 2 sts, rep from * around, ending last rep at **, join in first fpdc. (72 fpdc, 54 bpdc)

Rnd 14: Ch 1, fpdc dec around first 2 sts, *fpdc around each of next 2 sts, [fpdc dec around next 2 sts] twice, fpdc around each of next 2 sts, fpdc dec around next 2 sts, 2 bpdc around next bpdc, bpdc around each of next 7 bpdc, 2 bpdc around next bpdc**, fpdc dec around next 2 sts, rep from * around, ending last rep at **, join in first fpdc. (48 fpdc, 66 bpdc)

Rnd 15: Ch 1, fpdc dec around first 2 sts, [fpdc dec around next 2 sts] 3 times, *bpdc around each of next 11 bpdc**, [fpdc dec around next 2 sts] 4 times, rep from * around, ending last rep at **, join in first fpdc. (24 fpdc, 66 bpdc)

Rnd 16: Ch 1, bpdc in each of first 4 sts, *2 bpdc in next bpdc, bpdc in each of next 9 bpdc, 2 bpdc in next bpdc**, bpdc in each of next 4 sts, rep from * around, ending last rep at **, join in first bpdc. (102 bpdc)

Rnd 17: Ch 1, 2 bpdc around first bpdc, *bpdc around each of next 2 bpdc, 2 bpdc around next bpdc, bpdc around each of next 13 bpdc**, 2 bpdc around next bpdc, rep from * around, ending last rep at **, join in first bpdc. (114 bpdc)

Rnd 18: Ch 1, bpdc around each of first 6 bpdc, *2 bpdc around next bpdc, bpdc around each of next 11 bpdc, 2 bpdc around next bpdc**, bpdc around each of next 6 bpdc, rep from * around, ending last rep at **, join in first bpdc. (126 bpdc)

Rnd 19: Ch 1, 2 bpdc around first bpdc, *bpdc around each of next 4 bpdc, 2 bpdc around next bpdc, bpdc around each of next 15 bpdc**, 2 bpdc around next bpdc, rep from * around, ending last rep at **, join in first bpdc. (138 bpdc)

Rnd 20: Ch 1, fpdc around each of first 8 bpdc, *2 fpdc around next bpdc, fpdc around each of next 13 bpdc, 2 fpdc around next bpdc**, fpdc around each of next 8 bpdc, rep from * around, ending last rep at **, join in first fpdc. (150 fpdc)

Rnd 21: Ch 1, sc in first st, dtr in next st, *sc in next st, dtr in next st, rep from * around, join in first sc.

Rnd 22: Ch 1, dtr in first st, sc in next st, *dtr in next st, sc in next st, rep from * around, join in first dtr.

Rnd 23: Ch 1, sc in first st, dtr in next st, *sc in next st, dtr in next st, rep from * around, join in first sc.

Size Small/Medium Only

Rnd 24: Ch 3, dc in each of next 23 sc, 2 dc in next sc, *dc in each of next 24 sc, 2 dc in next sc, rep from * around, join in 3rd ch of beg ch-3. (156 dc)

Rnd 25: Ch 1, fpdc around each of first 25 dc, 2 fpdc around next dc, *fpdc around each of next 25 dc, 2 fpdc around next dc, rep from * around, join in first fpdc. (162 fpdc)

Rnd 26: Ch 1, fpdc around each of first 26 sts, 2 fpdc around next st, *fpdc around each of next 26 sts, 2 fpdc around next st, rep from * around, join in first fpdc. Fasten off. (168 fpdc)

Notes: Rows 27–45 form armholes, collar and body. Counting counterclockwise (or clockwise if left-handed) from first st of rnd 26, mark 99th st.

Row 27: Now working in rows, hold piece with RS facing, join yarn in marked st, **ch 3** *(see Pattern Notes)*, dc in each of next 13 fpdc, 2 dc in next fpdc, ch 27 *(armhole made)*, sk next 27 fpdc, 2 dc in next fpdc, [dc in each of next 27 fpdc, 2 dc in next fpdc] twice, ch 27 *(armhole made)*, sk next 27 fpdc, 2 dc in next fpdc, dc in each of next 14 fpdc, turn. *(92 dc, 54 chs)*

Note: *Following rows are worked in **back lps** only (see Stitch Guide).*

Row 28: Ch 3, dc in each of next 14 dc, 2 dc in next dc, [dc in each of next 28 sts, 2 dc in next st] 4 times, dc in each of next 14 dc, turn. *(151 dc)*

Row 29: Ch 3, dc in each of next 14 dc, 2 dc in next dc, [dc in each of next 29 sts, 2 dc in next st] 4 times, dc in each of next 15 dc, turn. *(156 dc)*

Row 30: Ch 3, dc in each of next 15 dc, 2 dc in next dc, [dc in each of next 30 sts, 2 dc in next st] 4 times, dc in each of next 15 dc, turn. *(161 dc)*

Row 31: Ch 3, dc in each of next 15 dc, 2 dc in next dc, [dc in each of next 31 sts, 2 dc in next st] 4 times, dc in each of next 16 dc, turn. *(166 dc)*

Row 32: Ch 3, dc in each of next 16 dc, 2 dc in next dc, [dc in each of next 32 sts, 2 dc in next st] 4 times, dc in each of next 16 dc, turn. *(171 dc)*

Row 33: Ch 3, dc in each of next 16 dc, 2 dc in next dc, [dc in each of next 33 sts, 2 dc in next st] 4 times, dc in each of next 17 dc, turn. *(176 dc)*

Row 34: Ch 3, dc in each of next 17 dc, 2 dc in next dc, [dc in each of next 34 sts, 2 dc in next st] 4 times, dc in each of next 17 dc, turn. *(181 dc)*

Row 35: Ch 3, dc in each of next 17 dc, 2 dc in next dc, [dc in each of next 35 sts, 2 dc in next st] 4 times, dc in each of next 18 dc, turn. *(186 dc)*

Row 36: Ch 3, dc in each of next 18 dc, 2 dc in next dc, [dc in each of next 36 sts, 2 dc in next st] 4 times, dc in each of next 18 dc, turn. *(191 dc)*

Row 37: Ch 3, dc in each of next 18 dc, 2 dc in next dc, [dc in each of next 37 sts, 2 dc in next st] 4 times, dc in each of next 19 dc, turn. *(196 dc)*

Row 38: Ch 3, dc in each of next 19 dc, 2 dc in next dc, [dc in each of next 38 sts, 2 dc in next st] 4 times, dc in each of next 19 dc, turn. *(201 dc)*

Row 39: Ch 3, dc in each of next 19 dc, 2 dc in next dc, [dc in each of next 39 sts, 2 dc in next st] 4 times, dc in each of next 20 dc, turn. *(206 dc)*

Row 40: Ch 3, dc in each of next 20 dc, 2 dc in next dc, [dc in each of next 40 sts, 2 dc in next st] 4 times, dc in each of next 20 dc, turn. *(211 dc)*

Row 41: Ch 3, dc in each of next 20 dc, 2 dc in next dc, [dc in each of next 41 sts, 2 dc in next st] 4 times, dc in each of next 21 dc, turn. *(216 dc)*

Row 42: Ch 3, dc in each of next 21 dc, 2 dc in next dc, [dc in each of next 42 sts, 2 dc in next st] 4 times, dc in each of next 21 dc, turn. *(221 dc)*

Row 43: Ch 3, dc in each of next 21 dc, 2 dc in next dc, [dc in each of next 43 sts, 2 dc in next st] 4 times, dc in each of next 22 dc, turn. *(226 dc)*

Row 44: Ch 3, dc in each of next 22 dc, 2 dc in next dc, [dc in each of next 44 sts, 2 dc in next st] 4 times, dc in each of next 22 dc, turn. *(231 dc)*

Row 45: Ch 3, dc in each of next 22 dc, 2 dc in next dc, [dc in each of next 45 sts, 2 dc in next st] 4 times, dc in each of next 23 dc, turn. *(236 dc)*

Edging
Rnd 46: Now working in rnd and in both lps, ch 1, sc in each st and end of each row, working 3 sc in each corner and 2 sc in end of each dc row around collar. Fasten off.

Size Large/X-Large Only
Rnd 24: Ch 1, dtr in first st, sc in next st, *dtr in next st, sc in next st, rep from * around, join in first dtr. *(150 sts)*

Rnd 25: Ch 1, sc in first st, dtr in next st, *sc in next st, dtr in next st, rep from * around, join in first sc.

Rnd 26: Ch 1, dtr in first st, sc in next st, *dtr in next st, sc in next st, rep from * around, join in first dtr.

Rnd 27: Ch 3, dc in each of next 23 sts, 2 dc in next st, *dc in each of next 24 dc, 2 dc in next st, rep from * around, join in 3rd ch of beg ch-3. *(156 dc)*

Rnd 28: Ch 1, fpdc around each of first 25 sts, 2 fpdc around next st, *fpdc around each of next 25 sts, 2 fpdc around next st, rep from * around, join in first fpdc. *(162 fpdc)*

Rnd 29: Ch 1, fpdc around first 26 sts, 2 fpdc around next st, *fpdc around each of next 26 sts, 2 fpdc around next st, rep from * around, join in first fpdc. *(168 fpdc)*

Rnd 30: Ch 1, fpdc around each of first 27 sts, 2 fpdc around next st, *fpdc around each of next 27 sts, 2 fpdc around next st, rep from * around, join in first fpdc. Fasten off. *(174 fpdc)*

Notes: *Rows 31–45 form armholes, collar and body. Counting counterclockwise (or clockwise if left-handed) from first st of rnd 30, mark 103rd st.*

Row 31: Now working in rows, hold piece with RS facing, join yarn in marked st, **ch 3** *(see Pattern Notes)*, dc in each of next 14 fpdc, 2 dc in next fpdc, ch 28 *(armhole made)*, sk next 28 fpdc, 2 dc in next fpdc, [dc in each of next 28 fpdc, 2 dc in next fpdc] twice, ch 28 *(armhole made)*, sk next 28 fpdc, 2 dc in next fpdc, dc in each of next 15 fpdc, turn. *(96 dc, 56 chs)*

Note: *Following rows are worked in **back lps** only (see Stitch Guide).*

Row 32: Ch 3, dc in each of next 15 dc, 2 dc in next dc, [dc in each of next 29 sts, 2 dc in next st] 4 times, dc in each of next 15 dc, turn. *(157 dc)*

Row 33: Ch 3, dc in each of next 16 dc, 2 dc in next dc, [dc in each of next 30 sts, 2 dc in next st] 4 times, dc in each of next 16 dc, turn. *(162 dc)*

Row 34: Ch 3, dc in each of next 16 dc, 2 dc in next dc, [dc in each of next 31 sts, 2 dc in next st] 4 times, dc in each of next 17 dc, turn. *(167 dc)*

Row 35: Ch 3, dc in each of next 17 dc, 2 dc in next dc, [dc in each of next 32 sts, 2 dc in next st] 4 times, dc in each of next 17 dc, turn. *(172 dc)*

Row 36: Ch 3, dc in each of next 17 dc, 2 dc in next dc, [dc in each of next 33 sts, 2 dc in next st] 4 times, dc in each of next 18 dc, turn. *(177 dc)*

Row 37: Ch 3, dc in each of next 18 dc, 2 dc in next dc, [dc in each of next 34 sts, 2 dc in next st] 4 times, dc in each of next 18 dc, turn. *(182 dc)*

Row 38: Ch 3, dc in each of next 18 dc, 2 dc in next dc, [dc in each of next 35 sts, 2 dc in next st] 4 times, dc in each of next 19 dc, turn. *(187 dc)*

Row 39: Ch 3, dc in each of next 19 dc, 2 dc in next dc, [dc in each of next 36 sts, 2 dc in next st] 4 times, dc in each of next 19 dc, turn. *(192 dc)*

Row 40: Ch 3, dc in each of next 19 dc, 2 dc in next dc, [dc in each of next 36 sts, 2 dc in next st] 4 times, dc in each of next 19 dc, turn. *(197 dc)*

Row 41: Ch 3, dc in each of next 20 dc, 2 dc in next dc, [dc in each of next 38 sts, 2 dc in next st] 4 times, dc in each of next 20 dc, turn. *(202 dc)*

Row 42: Ch 3, dc in each of next 20 dc, 2 dc in next dc, [dc in each of next 39 sts, 2 dc in next st] 4 times, dc in each of next 21 dc, turn. *(207 dc)*

Row 43: Ch 3, dc in each of next 21 dc, 2 dc in next dc, [dc in each of next 40 sts, 2 dc in next st] 4 times, dc in each of next 21 dc, turn. *(212 dc)*

Row 44: Ch 3, dc in each of next 21 dc, 2 dc in next dc, [dc in each of next 41 sts, 2 dc in next st] 4 times, dc in each of next 22 dc, turn. *(217 dc)*

Row 45: Ch 3, dc in each of next 22 dc, 2 dc in next dc, [dc in each of next 42 sts, 2 dc in next st] 4 times, dc in each of next 22 dc, turn. *(222 dc)*

Row 46: Ch 3, dc in each of next 22 dc, 2 dc in next dc, [dc in each of next 43 sts, 2 dc in next st] 4 times, dc in each of next 23 dc, turn. *(227 dc)*

Row 47: Ch 3, dc in each of next 23 dc, 2 dc in next dc, [dc in each of next 44 sts, 2 dc in next st] 4 times, dc in each of next 23 dc, turn. *(232 dc)*

Row 48: Ch 3, dc in each of next 23 dc, 2 dc in next dc, [dc in each of next 45 sts, 2 dc in next st] 4 times, dc in each of next 24 dc, turn. *(237 dc)*

Row 49: Ch 3, dc in each of next 24 dc, 2 dc in next dc, [dc in each of next 46 sts, 2 dc in next st] 4 times, dc in each of next 24 dc, turn. *(242 dc)*

Row 50: Ch 3, dc in each of next 24 dc, 2 dc in next dc, [dc in each of next 47 sts, 2 dc in next st] 4 times, dc in each of next 25 dc, turn. *(247 dc)*

Row 51: Ch 3, dc in each of next 25 dc, 2 dc in next dc, [dc in each of next 48 sts, 2 dc in next st] 4 times, dc in each of next 54 dc, turn. *(252 dc)*

Row 52: Ch 3, dc in each of next 25 dc, 2 dc in next dc, [dc in each of next 49 sts, 2 dc in next st] 4 times, dc in each of next 25 dc, turn. *(257 dc)*

Edging

Rnd 53: Now working in rnds and in both lps, ch 1, sc in each st and end of each row, working 3 sc in each corner and 2 sc in end of each dc row around collar. Fasten off.

Size 2X-Large/3X-Large Only

Rnds 24–29: Work same as rnds 24–29 of Large/X-large.

Rnd 30: Ch 1, fpdc around each of first 27 sts, 2 fpdc around next st, *fpdc around each of next 27 sts, 2 fpdc around next st, rep from * around, join in first fpdc. *(174 fpdc)*

Rnd 31: Ch 1, fpdc around each of first 28 sts, 2 fpdc around next st, *fpdc around each of next 28 sts, 2 fpdc around next st, rep from * around, join in first fpdc. Fasten off. *(180 fpdc)*

Notes: *Rows 32–55 form armholes, collar and body. Counting counterclockwise (or clockwise if left-handed) from first st of rnd 31, mark 107th st.*

Row 32: Now working in rows, hold piece with RS facing, join yarn in marked st, **ch 3** *(see Pattern Notes)*, dc in each of next 15 fpdc, 2 dc in next fpdc, ch 29 *(armhole made)*, sk next 29 fpdc, 2 dc in next fpdc, [dc in each of next 29 fpdc, 2 dc in next fpdc] twice, ch 29 *(armhole made)*, sk next 29 fpdc, 2 dc in next fpdc, dc in each of next 16 fpdc, turn. *(100 dc, 58 chs)*

Note: *Following rows are worked in* **back lps** *only (see Stitch Guide).*

Row 33: Ch 3, dc in each of next 16 dc, 2 dc in next dc, [dc in each of next 30 sts, 2 dc in next st] 4 times, dc in each of next 16 dc, turn. *(163 dc)*

Row 34: Ch 3, dc in each of next 16 dc, 2 dc in next dc, [dc in each of next 31 sts, 2 dc in next st] 4 times, dc in each of next 17 dc, turn. *(168 dc)*

Row 35: Ch 3, dc in each of next 17 dc, 2 dc in next dc, [dc in each of next 32 sts, 2 dc in next st] 4 times, dc in each of next 17 dc, turn. *(173 dc)*

Row 36: Ch 3, dc in each of next 17 dc, 2 dc in next dc, [dc in each of next 33 sts, 2 dc in next st] 4 times, dc in each of next 18 dc, turn. *(178 dc)*

Row 37: Ch 3, dc in each of next 18 dc, 2 dc in next dc, [dc in each of next 34 sts, 2 dc in next st] 4 times, dc in each of next 18 dc, turn. *(183 dc)*

Row 38: Ch 3, dc in each of next 18 dc, 2 dc in next dc, [dc in each of next 35 sts, 2 dc in next st] 4 times, dc in each of next 19 dc, turn. *(188 dc)*

Row 39: Ch 3, dc in each of next 19 dc, 2 dc in next dc, [dc in each of next 36 sts, 2 dc in next st] 4 times, dc in each of next 19 dc, turn. *(193 dc)*

Row 40: Ch 3, dc in each of next 19 dc, 2 dc in next dc, [dc in each of next 37 sts, 2 dc in next st] 4 times, dc in each of next 20 dc, turn. *(198 dc)*

Row 41: Ch 3, dc in each of next 20 dc, 2 dc in next dc, [dc in each of next 38 sts, 2 dc in next st] 4 times, dc in each of next 20 dc, turn. *(203 dc)*

Row 42: Ch 3, dc in each of next 20 dc, 2 dc in next dc, [dc in each of next 39 sts, 2 dc in next st] 4 times, dc in each of next 21 dc, turn. *(208 dc)*

Row 43: Ch 3, dc in each of next 21 dc, 2 dc in next dc, [dc in each of next 40 sts, 2 dc in next st] 4 times, dc in each of next 21 dc, turn. *(213 dc)*

Row 44: Ch 3, dc in each of next 21 dc, 2 dc in next dc, [dc in each of next 41 sts, 2 dc in next st] 4 times, dc in each of next 22 dc, turn. *(218 dc)*

Row 45: Ch 3, dc in each of next 22 dc, 2 dc in next dc, [dc in each of next 42 sts, 2 dc in next st] 4 times, dc in each of next 22 dc, turn. *(223 dc)*

Row 46: Ch 3, dc in each of next 22 dc, 2 dc in next dc, [dc in each of next 43 sts, 2 dc in next st] 4 times, dc in each of next 23 dc, turn. *(228 dc)*

Row 47: Ch 3, dc in each of next 23 dc, 2 dc in next dc, [dc in each of next 44 sts, 2 dc in next st] 4 times, dc in each of next 23 dc, turn. *(233 dc)*

Row 48: Ch 3, dc in each of next 23 dc, 2 dc in next dc, [dc in each of next 45 sts, 2 dc in next st] 4 times, dc in each of next 24 dc, turn. *(238 dc)*

Row 49: Ch 3, dc in each of next 24 dc, 2 dc in next dc, [dc in each of next 46 sts, 2 dc in next st] 4 times, dc in each of next 24 dc, turn. *(243 dc)*

Row 50: Ch 3, dc in each of next 24 dc, 2 dc in next dc, [dc in each of next 47 sts, 2 dc in next st] 4 times, dc in each of next 25 dc, turn. *(248 dc)*

Row 51: Ch 3, dc in each of next 25 dc, 2 dc in next dc, [dc in each of next 48 sts, 2 dc in next st] 4 times, dc in each of next 25 dc, turn. *(253 dc)*

Row 52: Ch 3, dc in each of next 25 dc, 2 dc in next dc, [dc in each of next 49 sts, 2 dc in next st] 4 times, dc in each of next 26 dc, turn. *(258 dc)*

Row 53: Ch 3, dc in each of next 26 dc, 2 dc in next dc, [dc in each of next 50 sts, 2 dc in next st] 4 times, dc in each of next 26 dc, turn. *(263 dc)*

Row 54: Ch 3, dc in each of next 26 dc, 2 dc in next dc, [dc in each of next 51 sts, 2 dc in next st] 4 times, dc in each of next 27 dc, turn. *(268 dc)*

Row 55: Ch 3, dc in each of next 27 dc, 2 dc in next dc, [dc in each of next 52 sts, 2 dc in next st] 4 times, dc in each of next 27 dc, turn. *(273 dc)*

Edging

Rnd 56: Now working in rnds and in both lps, ch 1, sc in each st and end of each row, working 3 sc in each corner and 2 sc in end of each dc row around collar. Fasten off. ●

Flower Handbag

Skill Level

 INTERMEDIATE

Finished Measurements

18 inches wide x 13 inches deep

Materials

- Size 3 crochet cotton:
    1,050 yds cream
    450 yds brown
- Size D/3/3.25mm crochet hook or size needed to obtain gauge
- Tapestry needle
- 1 set of brown double rolled microfiber handles by Everything Mary

Gauge

10 sts = 2 inches; 6 rows = 2 inches

Take time to check gauge.

Gauge Swatch

Row 1: Ch 13, dc in 4th ch from hook and in each rem ch across, turn. *(10 dc)*

Row 2: Ch 3 *(does not count as first dc)*, fpdc around each st across, turn.

Row 3: Ch 3, bpdc around each st across, turn.

Rows 4 & 5: Rep rows 2 and 3.

Row 6: Rep row 2.

Pattern Notes

Weave in loose ends as work progresses.

Join with slip stitch as indicated unless otherwise stated.

Chain-3 at beginning of round worked in double crochet counts as first double crochet unless otherwise stated.

Special Stitches

Front post double crochet dec (fpdc dec): *Yo, insert hook from front to back to front around post of next dc, yo, pull up lp, yo, draw through 2 lps on hook, rep from * once, yo and draw through all 3 lps on hook.

Back post double crochet dec (bpdc dec): *Yo, insert hook from back to front to back around post of next dc, yo, pull up lp, yo, draw through 2 lps on hook, rep from * once, yo and draw through all 3 lps on hook.

Handbag

Hexagon
Make 15.

Rnd 1 (RS): With brown, ch 4, **join** (see Pattern Notes) in first ch to form ring, ch 1, 6 sc in ring, join in first sc. (6 sc)

Rnd 2: Ch 1, (sc, **dtr**—see Stitch Guide) in each sc around, join in first sc. (6 sc, 6 dtr)

Rnd 3: Ch 1, (sc, dtr) in each st around, join in first sc. Change color to cream by drawing lp through; cut brown. (12 sc, 12 dtr)

Rnd 4: Ch 3 (see Pattern Notes), dc in each of next 2 sts, 2 dc in next st, *dc in each of next 3 sts, 2 dc in next st, rep from * around, join in 3rd ch of beg ch 3. (30 dc)

Rnd 5: Ch 1, 2 **fpdc** (see Stitch Guide) around same beg ch-3 as joining, 2 fpdc around each of next 2 dc, 2 sc in each of next 2 dc, *2 fpdc around each of next 3 dc, 2 sc in each of next 2 dc, rep from * around, join in first fpdc. (36 fpdc, 24 sc)

Rnd 6: Ch 1, 2 fpdc around first fpdc, 2 fpdc around each of next 5 fpdc, *2 sc in next sc, sc in each of next 2 sc, 2 sc in next sc, 2 fpdc around each of next 6 fpdc, rep from * 4 times, 2 sc in next sc, sc in each of next 2 sc, 2 sc in next sc, join in first fpdc. (72 fpdc, 36 sc)

Rnd 7: Ch 1, **fpdc dec** (see Special Stitches) around first 2 sts, [fpdc dec around next 2 sts] 5 times, *2 sc in next sc, sc in each of next 4 sc, 2 sc in next sc**, [fpdc dec around next 2 sts] 6 times, rep from * around, ending last rep at **, join in first st. (36 fpdc, 48 sc)

Rnd 8: Ch 1, fpdc dec around first 3 sts, fpdc dec around next 3 sts, *2 sc in next sc, sc in each of next 6 sc, 2 sc in next sc**, [fpdc dec around next 3 sts] twice, rep from * around, ending last rep at **, join in first st. (12 fpdc, 60 sc)

Rnd 9: Ch 1, *bpdc dec (see Special Stitches) around first 2 sts, sc in each of next 10 sc, *bpdc dec around next 2 sts, sc in each of next 10 sc, rep from * around, join in first st. (6 bpdc, 60 sc)

Rnd 10: Ch 1, 2 sc in first st, sc in each of next 10 sts, *2 sc in next st, sc in each of next 10 sts, rep from * around, join in first sc. Change to brown by drawing lp through; cut cream. (72 sc)

Rnd 11: Ch 1, sc in first sc, dtr in next sc, *sc in next sc, dtr in next sc, rep from * around, join in first sc.

Rnd 12: Ch 1, dtr in first sc, sc in next dtr, *dtr in next sc, sc in next dtr, rep from * around, join in first dtr. Change color to cream by drawing lp through; cut brown.

Rnd 13: Ch 3, 3 dc in next st, *dc in each of next 11 sts, 3 dc in next st, rep from * around to last 10 sts, dc in each of last 10 sts, join in first dc. Fasten off. (84 dc)

Assembly

Block Hexagons by soaking them in cool water until thoroughly wet. Gently squeeze out excess water and pin on a flat surface. Remove only when completely dry.

Referring to Assembly Diagram arrange Hexagons. Referring to photo, sl st Hexagons together. Fold piece on red lines, matching each side letter to its correspondent letter. Sew sides tog with sl sts through both thicknesses.

Sew handles to each side of Handbag. ●

Flower Handbag
Assembly Diagram

Daisy Blanket

Skill Level

 INTERMEDIATE

Finished Measurements

40 inches wide x 58 inches long

Materials

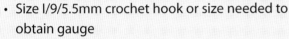

- Medium (worsted) weight acrylic yarn:
  49 oz/3,206 yds/1400g off-white
- Size I/9/5.5mm crochet hook or size needed to obtain gauge
- Tapestry needle

Gauge

7 sts = 2 inches; 5 rows = 2 inches

Take time to check gauge.

Gauge Swatch

Row 1: Ch 10, dc in 4th ch from hook and in each rem ch across, turn. *(7 dc)*

Row 2: Ch 3 *(does not count as first dc)*, fpdc around each st across, turn.

Row 3: Ch 3, bpdc around each st across, turn.

Rows 4 & 5: Rep rows 2 and 3.

Pattern Notes

In some rounds throughout pattern, such as rounds 5 and 6, Motif tends to cup or ruffle. This is not an error in instructions. Subsequent rounds will even out the cupping or ruffling and create the embossed look.

Weave in loose ends as work progresses.

Join with slip stitch as indicated unless otherwise stated.

Chain-3 at beginning of round or row worked in double crochet counts as first double crochet unless otherwise stated.

Chain-3 at beginning of round worked in front post double crochet counts as first front post double crochet unless otherwise stated.

Chain-3 at beginning of round worked in back post double crochet counts as first back post double crochet unless otherwise stated.

Special Stitches

V-stitch (V-st): (Dc, ch 1, dc) in indicated st.

Front post double crochet dec (fpdc dec): *Yo, insert hook from front to back to front around post of next dc, yo, pull up lp, yo, draw through 2 lps on hook, rep from * once, yo and draw through all 3 lps on hook.

Back post double crochet dec (bpdc dec): *Yo, insert hook from back to front to back around post of next dc, yo, pull up lp, yo, draw through 2 lps on hook, rep from * once, yo and draw through all 3 lps on hook.

Blanket

Hexagon Motif
Make 13.

Rnd 1 (RS): Ch 4, **join** (see Pattern Notes) in first ch to form ring, ch 1, 6 sc in ring, join in first sc. (6 sc)

Rnd 2: Ch 1, (sc, **dtr**—see Stitch Guide) in each sc around, join in first sc. (6 dtr, 6 sc)

Rnd 3: Ch 1, dtr in first sc, (sc, dtr) in next st, sc in next sc, (dtr, sc) in next st, [dtr in next st, (sc, dtr) in next st, sc in next st, (dtr, sc) in next st] twice, join in first dtr. (9 dtr, 9 sc)

Rnd 4: Ch 1, sc in first dtr, dtr in next st, (sc, dtr) in next st, [sc in next st, dtr in next st, (sc, dtr) in next st] 5 times, join in first sc. (12 dtr, 12 sc)

Rnd 5: Ch 3 (see Pattern Notes), dc in each of next 2 sts, 2 dc in next st, [dc in each of next 3 sts, 2 dc in next st] 5 times, join in 3rd ch of beg ch-3. (30 dc)

Rnd 6: Ch 1, **fpdc** (see Stitch Guide) around beg ch-3, fpdc around next dc, *ch 1, fpdc around each of next 2 dc, 3 **bpdc** (see Stitch Guide) around next dc**, fpdc around each of next 2 dc, rep from * around, ending last rep at **, join in first fpdc. (24 fpdc, 18 bpdc, 6 ch-1 sps)

Rnd 7: Ch 1, fpdc around first fpdc, fpdc around next fpdc, *V-st (see Special Stitches) in next ch-1 sp, fpdc around each of next 2 fpdc, 2 bpdc around next bpdc, bpdc around next bpdc, 2 bpdc around next bpdc**, fpdc around each of next 2 fpdc, rep from * around, ending last rep at **, join in first fpdc. (30 bpdc, 24 fpdc, 6 V-sts)

Rnd 8: Ch 1, fpdc around first fpdc, fpdc around each of next 2 sts, *V-st in next ch-1 sp, fpdc around each of next 3 sts, 2 bpdc around next bpdc, bpdc around each of next 3 bpdc, 2 bpdc around next bpdc**, fpdc around each of next 3 sts, rep from * around, ending last rep at **, join in first fpdc. (42 bpdc, 36 fpdc, 6 V-sts)

Rnd 9: Ch 1, fpdc around first fpdc, fpdc around each of next 3 sts, *V-st in next ch-1 sp, fpdc around each of next 4 sts, 2 bpdc around next bpdc, bpdc around each of next 5 bpdc, 2 bpdc around next bpdc**, fpdc around next 4 sts, rep from * around, ending last rep at **, join in first fpdc. (54 bpdc, 48 fpdc, 6 V-sts)

Rnd 10: Ch 1, fpdc around first fpdc, fpdc around each of next 4 sts, *V-st in next ch-1 sp, fpdc around each of next 5 sts, 2 bpdc around next bpdc, bpdc around each of next 7 bpdc, 2 bpdc around next bpdc**, fpdc around each of next 5 sts, rep from * around, ending last rep at **, join in first fpdc. (66 bpdc, 60 fpdc, 6 V-sts)

Rnd 11: Ch 1, **fpdc dec** (see Special Stitches) around first 2 sts, *fpdc around each of next 2 sts, [fpdc dec around next 2 sts] twice, fpdc around each of next 2 fpdc, fpdc dec around next 2 sts, bpdc around each of next 11 bpdc**, fpdc around next 2 sts, rep from * around, ending last rep at **, join in first fpdc. (66 bpdc, 48 fpdc)

Rnd 12: Ch 1, fpdc dec around first 2 sts, [fpdc dec around next 2 sts] 3 times, *2 bpdc around next bpdc, bpdc around each of next 9 bpdc, 2 bpdc around next bpdc**, [fpdc dec around next 2 sts] 4 times, rep from * around, ending last rep at **, join in first fpdc. (78 bpdc, 24 fpdc)

Rnd 13: Ch 1, fpdc dec around first 2 sts, fpdc dec around next 2 sts, bpdc around each of next 13 bpdc, *[fpdc dec around next 2 sts] twice, bpdc around each of next 13 bpdc, rep from * around, join in first fpdc. (78 bpdc, 12 fpdc)

Rnd 14: Ch 1, **bpdc dec** (see Special Stitches) around first 2 sts, *2 bpdc around next bpdc, bpdc around each of next 11 bpdc, 2 bpdc around next bpdc**, bpdc dec around next 2 sts, rep from * around, ending last rep at **, join in first bpdc. (96 bpdc)

Rnd 15: Ch 1, 3 fpdc around first bpdc, fpdc around each of next 15 bpdc, *3 fpdc around next st, fpdc around each of next 15 bpdc, rep from * around, join in first fpdc. (108 fpdc)

Rnd 16: Ch 1, sc in first st, dtr in next st, *sc in next st, dtr in next st, rep from * around, join in first sc. (54 dtr, 54 sc)

Rnd 17: Ch 1, dtr in first st, sc in next st, *dtr in next st, sc in next st, rep from * around, join in first dtr.

Rnd 18: Ch 3, [3 dc in next st, dc in each of next 17 sts] 5 times, 3 dc in next st, dc in each of next 16 dc, join in 3rd ch of beg ch-3. Fasten off. (120 dc)

Half Hexagon Motif
Make 4.

Row 1 (WS): Ch 4, join in first ch to form ring, ch 1, 3 sc in ring, join in first sc, turn. (3 sc)

Row 2 (RS): Ch 1, (sc, dtr) in each sc across, sl st in same sc as last dtr worked, turn. (3 sc, 3 dtr)

Note: On row 3, when crocheting dtr, push st through work, so texture can show on RS of work.

Row 3: Ch 1, dtr in first st, (sc, dtr) in next st, sc in next st, (dtr, sc) in next st, dtr in next st, (sc, dtr, sl st) in last st, turn. (5 dtr, 4 sc)

Row 4: Ch 1, sc in first dtr, dtr in next st, (sc, dtr) in next st, sc in next st, dtr in next st, (sc, dtr) in next st, sc in next st, dtr in next st, (sc, dtr, sl st) in last st, turn. (6 dtr, 6 sc)

Row 5: Ch 3 (see Pattern Notes), sk first dtr, dc in each of next 2 sts, 2 dc in next st, [dc in each of next 3 sts, 2 dc in next st] twice, turn. (15 dc)

Row 6: Ch 1, fpdc around first dc, fpdc around next dc, 3 bpdc around next dc, [fpdc around each of next 2 dc, ch 1, fpdc around each of next 2 dc, 3 bpdc around next dc] twice, fpdc around each of next 2 dc, turn. (12 fpdc, 9 bpdc, 2 ch-1 sps)

Row 7: Ch 3 (does not count as a st), bpdc around first st, 2 bpdc around next st, 2 fpdc around next st, fpdc around next st, 2 fpdc around next st, [bpdc around each of next 2 sts, V-st in next ch-1 sp, bpdc around each of next 2 sts, 2 fpdc around next st, fpdc around next st, 2 fpdc around next st] twice, 2 bpdc around next st, bpdc around next st, turn. (2 V-sts, 14 bpdc, 15 fpdc)

Row 8: Ch 1, fpdc around first st, fpdc around next st, 2 fpdc around next st, 2 bpdc around next st, bpdc around each of next 3 sts, 2 bpdc around next st, [fpdc around each of next 3 sts, V-st in next ch-1 sp, fpdc around each of next 3 sts, 2 bpdc around next st, bpdc around each of next 3 sts, 2 bpdc around next st] twice, 2 fpdc around next st, fpdc around each of next 2 sts, turn. (2 V-sts, 21 bpdc, 20 fpdc)

Row 9: Ch 3 (does not count as a st), bpdc around first st, bpdc around each of next 2 sts, 2 bpdc around next st, 2 fpdc around next st, fpdc around each of next 5 sts, 2 fpdc around next st, [bpdc around each of next 4 sts, V-st in next ch-1 sp, bpdc around each of next 4 sts, 2 fpdc around next st, fpdc around each of next 5 sts, 2 fpdc around next st] twice, 2 bpdc around next st, bpdc around each of next 3 sts, turn. (2 V-sts, 26 bpdc, 27 fpdc)

Row 10: Ch 1, fpdc around first st, fpdc around each of next 3 sts, 2 fpdc around next st, 2 bpdc around next st, bpdc around each of next 7 sts, 2 bpdc around next st, [fpdc around each of next 5 sts, V-st in next ch-1 sp, fpdc around each of next 5 sts, 2 bpdc around next st, bpdc around each of next 7 sts, 2 bpdc around next st] twice, 2 fpdc around next st, fpdc around each of next 4 sts, turn. (2 V-sts, 33 bpdc, 32 fpdc)

Row 11: Ch 3 *(does not count as a st)*, bpdc around first st, bpdc around next st, [bpdc dec around next 2 sts] twice, fpdc around each of next 11 sts, *bpdc dec around next 2 sts, bpdc around each of next 2 sts, [bpdc dec around next 2 sts] twice, bpdc around each of next 2 sts, bpdc dec around next 2 sts, fpdc around each of next 11 sts, rep from * once, [bpdc dec around next 2 sts] twice, bpdc around each of next 2 sts, turn. *(24 bpdc, 33 fpdc)*

Row 12: Ch 1, [fpdc dec around next 2 sts] twice, 2 bpdc around next st, bpdc around each of next 9 sts, 2 bpdc around next st, *[fpdc dec around next 2 sts] 4 times, 2 bpdc around next st, bpdc around each of next 9 sts, 2 bpdc around next st, rep from * once, [fpdc dec around next 2 sts] twice, turn. *(39 bpdc, 12 fpdc)*

Row 13: Ch 3 *(does not count as a st)*, bpdc dec around first 2 sts, fpdc around each of next 13 sts, *[bpdc dec around next 2 sts] twice, fpdc around each of next 13 sts, rep from * once, bpdc dec around next 2 sts, turn. *(6 bpdc, 39 fpdc)*

Row 14: Ch 3 *(see Pattern Notes)*, [2 bpdc around next st, bpdc around each of next 11 sts, 2 bpdc around next st, bpdc dec around next 2 sts] twice, 2 bpdc around next st, bpdc around each of next 11 sts, 2 bpdc around next st, bpdc around next st, turn. *(49 bpdc)*

Row 15: Ch 3, bpdc around each of next 15 sts, [3 bpdc around next st, bpdc around each of next 15 sts] twice, bpdc around next st, turn. *(53 bpdc)*

Row 16: Ch 1, sc around first st, *dtr around next st, sc in next st, rep from * across, turn.

Row 17: Ch 1, dtr in first st, sc in next st, *dtr in next st, sc in next st, rep from * across to last st, (dtr, sl st) in last st, turn.

Row 18: Sl st in first st, ch 3, dc in each of next 16 sts, [3 dc in next st, dc in each of next 17 sts] twice. *(57 dc)*

Assembly
Block Motifs before assembly. Referring to Assembly Diagram, sl st Motifs tog.

Edging
Rnd 1: With RS of Blanket facing, join yarn in any corner, ch 1, sc in each st around and 2 sc in each Hexagon point, join in first sc. Fasten off. ●

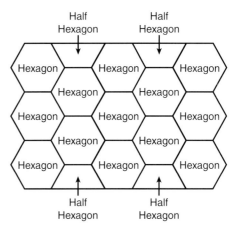

Daisy Blanket
Assembly Diagram

Garden Handbag

Skill Level

 INTERMEDIATE

Finished Measurements

16 inches wide x 16 inches deep, excluding Handles

Materials

- Medium (worsted) weight acrylic yarn:
  21 oz/1,536 yds/600g tan
- Sizes H/8/5mm and I/9/5.5mm crochet hooks or sizes needed to obtain gauge
- Tapestry needle
- Large toggle button (optional)

Gauge

Size I hook: 7 sts = 2 inches; 5 rows = 2 inches

Take time to check gauge.

Gauge Swatch

Row 1: Ch 10, dc in 4th ch from hook and in each rem ch across, turn. *(7 dc)*

Row 2: Ch 3 *(does not count as first dc)*, fpdc around each st across, turn.

Row 3: Ch 3, bpdc around each st across, turn.

Rows 4 & 5: Rep rows 2 and 3.

Pattern Notes

Weave in loose ends as work progresses.

Join with slip stitch as indicated unless otherwise stated.

Chain-3 at beginning of round worked in double crochet counts as first double crochet unless otherwise stated.

Chain-3 at beginning of round worked in back post double crochet and front post double crochet counts as first back post double crochet unless otherwise stated.

Special Stitches

V-stitch (V-st): (Dc, ch 1, dc) in indicated st.

Back post double crochet dec (bpdc dec): *Yo, insert hook from back to front to back around post of next dc, yo, pull up lp, yo, draw through 2 lps on hook, rep from * once, yo and draw through all 3 lps on hook.

Front post double crochet dec (fpdc dec): *Yo, insert hook from front to back to front around post of next dc, yo, pull up lp, yo, draw through 2 lps on hook, rep from * once, yo and draw through all 3 lps on hook.

Handbag

Motif
Make 2.

Rnd 1 (RS): With I hook, ch 4, **join** *(see Pattern Notes)* in first ch to form ring, **ch 3** *(see Pattern Notes)*, 15 dc in ring, join in first sc. *(16 dc)*

Rnd 2: Ch 3 *(see Pattern Notes)*, 2 **bpdc** *(see Stitch Guide)* around same beg ch-3 as joining, ***fpdc** (see Stitch Guide)* around next dc, 3 bpdc around next dc, (fpdc, ch 1, fpdc) around next dc**, 3 bpdc around next dc, rep from * around, ending last rep at **, join in 3rd ch of beg ch-3. *(24 bpdc, 12 fpdc)*

Rnd 3: Ch 3, bpdc around each of next 2 bpdc, *fpdc around next fpdc, bpdc around each of next 3 bpdc, fpdc around next fpdc, **V-st** *(see Special Stitches)* in next ch-1 sp, fpdc around next fpdc**, bpdc around each of next 3 bpdc, rep from * around, ending last rep at **, join in 3rd ch of beg ch-3. *(4 V-sts, 24 bpdc, 12 fpdc)*

Rnd 4: Ch 3, bpdc around same beg ch-3 as joining, *bpdc around next bpdc, 2 bpdc around next bpdc, fpdc around next fpdc, 2 bpdc around next bpdc,

bpdc around next bpdc, 2 bpdc around next bpdc, fpdc around each of next 2 sts, V-st in next ch-1 sp, fpdc around each of next 2 sts**, 2 bpdc around next bpdc, rep from * around, ending last rep at **, join in 3rd ch of beg ch-3. *(4 V-sts, 40 bpdc, 20 fpdc)*

Rnd 5: Ch 3, bpdc around each of next 4 bpdc, *fpdc around next dc, bpdc around each of next 5 bpdc, fpdc around each of next 3 sts, V-st in next ch-1 sp, fpdc around each of next 3 sts**, bpdc around each of next 5 bpdc, rep from * around, ending last rep at **, join in 3rd ch of beg ch-3. *(4 V-sts, 40 bpdc, 28 fpdc)*

Rnd 6: Ch 3, bpdc around same beg ch-3 as joining, *bpdc around each of next 3 bpdc, 2 bpdc around next bpdc, fpdc around next fpdc, 2 bpdc around next bpdc, bpdc around each of next 3 bpdc, 2 bpdc around next bpdc, fpdc around each of next 4 sts, V-st in next ch-1 sp, fpdc around each of next 4 sts**, 2 bpdc in next bpdc, rep from * around, ending last rep at **, join in 3rd ch of beg ch-3. *(4 V-sts, 56 bpdc, 36 fpdc)*

Rnd 7: Ch 3, bpdc around each of next 6 bpdc, *fpdc around next fpdc, bpdc around each of next 7 bpdc, fpdc around each of next 5 sts, V-st in next ch-1 sp, fpdc around each of next 5 sts**, bpdc around each of next 7 bpdc, rep from * around, ending last rep at **, join in 3rd ch of beg ch-3. *(4 V-sts, 56 bpdc, 44 fpdc)*

Rnd 8: Sl st around next bpdc, ch 3, *bpdc around each of next 3 bpdc, **bpdc dec** *(see Special Stitches)* around next 2 bpdc, (fpdc, ch 1, 5 fpdc, ch 1, fpdc) around next fpdc, bpdc dec around next 2 bpdc, bpdc in next 3 bpdc, bpdc dec around next 2 bpdc, **fpdc dec** *(see Special Stitches)* around next 2 fpdc, fpdc around each of next 2 fpdc, [fpdc dec around next 2 fpdc] twice, fpdc around each of next 2 fpdc, fpdc dec around next 2 fpdc**, bpdc dec around next 2 bpdc, rep from * around, ending last rep at **, join in 3rd ch of beg ch-3. *(40 bpdc, 60 fpdc, 8 ch-1 sps)*

Rnd 9: Ch 3, bpdc around each of next 4 bpdc, *fpdc around next fpdc, V-st in next ch-1 sp, fpdc around next fpdc, [3 bpdc around next fpdc, fpdc around next fpdc] twice, V-st in next ch-1 sp, fpdc around next fpdc, bpdc around each of next 5 bpdc, [fpdc dec around next 2 fpdc] 4 times**, bpdc around each of next 5 bpdc, rep from * around, ending last rep at **, join in 3rd ch of beg ch-3. *(8 V-sts, 64 bpdc, 36 fpdc)*

Rnd 10: Sl st around next bpdc, ch 3, *bpdc around next bpdc, bpdc dec around next 2 bpdc, fpdc around each of next 2 sts, V-st in next ch-1 sp, fpdc around each of next 2 sts, bpdc around each of next 3 bpdc, fpdc around next fpdc, bpdc around each of next 3 bpdc, fpdc around each of next 2 sts, V-st in next ch-1 sp, fpdc around each of next 2 sts, bpdc dec around next 2 sts, bpdc around next bpdc, bpdc dec around next 2 sts, [fpdc dec around next 2 sts] twice**, bpdc dec around next 2 bpdc, rep from * around, ending last rep at **, join in 3rd ch of beg ch-3. *(8 V-sts, 48 bpdc, 44 fpdc)*

Rnd 11: Ch 3, bpdc around each of next 2 bpdc, *fpdc around each of next 3 sts, V-st around next ch-1 sp, fpdc around each of next 3 sts, 2 bpdc around next bpdc, bpdc around next bpdc, 2 bpdc around next bpdc, fpdc around next fpdc, 2 bpdc around next bpdc, bpdc around next bpdc, 2 bpdc around next bpdc, fpdc around each of next 3 sts, V-st in next ch-1 sp, fpdc around each of next 3 sts, bpdc around each of next 3 bpdc, fpdc dec around next 2 sts**, bpdc around each of next 3 bpdc, rep from * around, ending last rep at **, join in 3rd ch of beg ch-3. *(8 V-sts, 64 bpdc, 56 fpdc)*

Rnd 12: Ch 3, bpdc around same beg ch-3 as joining, *bpdc around next bpdc, 2 bpdc around next bpdc, fpdc around each of next 4 sts, V-st in next ch-1 sp, fpdc around each of next 4 sts, bpdc around each of next 5 bpdc, fpdc around next fpdc, bpdc around each of next 5 bpdc, fpdc around each of next 4 sts, V-st in next ch-1 sp, fpdc around each of next 4 sts, 2 bpdc around next bpdc, bpdc around next bpdc, 2 bpdc around next bpdc, fpdc around next fpdc**, 2 bpdc around next bpdc, rep from * around, ending last rep at **, join in 3rd ch of beg ch-3. *(8 V-sts, 80 bpdc, 72 fpdc)*

Rnd 13: Ch 3, bpdc around each of next 4 bpdc, *fpdc around each of next 5 sts, V-st in next ch-1 sp, fpdc around each of next 5 sts, 2 bpdc around next bpdc, bpdc around each of next 3 bpdc, 2 bpdc around next bpdc, fpdc around next fpdc, 2 bpdc around next bpdc, bpdc around each of next 3 bpdc, 2 bpdc around next bpdc, fpdc around each of next 5 fpdc, V-st in next ch-1 sp, fpdc around each of next 5 fpdc, bpdc around each of next 5 bpdc, fpdc around next fpdc**, bpdc around each of next 5 bpdc, rep from * around, ending last rep at **, join in 3rd ch of beg ch-3. *(8 V-sts, 96 bpdc, 88 fpdc)*

Rnd 14: Ch 3, bpdc around same beg ch-3 as joining, *bpdc around each of next 3 bpdc, 2 bpdc around next bpdc, fpdc dec around next 2 sts, fpdc around each of next 2 fpdc, [fpdc dec around next 2 sts] twice, fpdc around each of next 2 fpdc, fpdc dec around next 2 sts, bpdc around each of next 7 bpdc, (fpdc, ch 1, fpdc) around next fpdc, bpdc around each of next 7 bpdc, fpdc dec around next 2 sts, fpdc around each of next 2 fpdc, [fpdc dec around next 2 sts] twice, fpdc around each of next 2 fpdc, fpdc dec around next 2 sts, 2 bpdc around next bpdc, bpdc around each of next 3 bpdc, 2 bpdc around next bpdc, (fpdc, ch 1, fpdc) around next fpdc**, 2 bpdc around next bpdc, rep from * around, ending last rep at **, join in 3rd ch of beg ch-3. *(112 bpdc, 80 fpdc, 8 ch-1 sps)*

Rnd 15: Ch 3, bpdc around each of next 6 bpdc, *[fpdc dec around next 2 sts] 4 times, bpdc dec around next 2 sts, bpdc around each of next 3 sts, bpdc dec around next 2 sts, fpdc around next fpdc, V-st in next ch-1 sp, fpdc around next fpdc, bpdc dec around next 2 sts, bpdc around each of next 3 sts, bpdc dec around next 2 sts, [fpdc dec around next 2 sts] 4 times, bpdc around each of next 7 bpdc, fpdc around next fpdc, V-st in next ch-1 sp, fpdc around next fpdc**, bpdc around each of next 7 bpdc, rep from * around, ending last rep at **, join in 3rd ch of beg ch-3. *(8 V-sts, 96 bpdc, 48 fpdc)*

Rnd 16: Sl st around next bpdc, ch 3, *bpdc around each of next 3 bpdc, bpdc dec around next 2 sts, [fpdc dec around next 2 sts] twice, bpdc around each of next 5 bpdc, fpdc around each of next 2 fpdc,

V-st in next ch-1 sp, fpdc around each of next 2 fpdc, bpdc around each of next 5 bpdc, [fpdc dec around next 2 sts] twice, bpdc dec around next 2 sts, bpdc around each of next 3 bpdc, bpdc dec around next 2 sts, fpdc around each of next 2 fpdc, V-st in next ch-1 sp, fpdc around each of next 2 fpdc**, bpdc dec around next 2 sts, rep from * around, ending last rep at **, join in 3rd ch of beg ch-3. (8 V-sts, 80 bpdc, 48 fpdc)

Rnd 17: Ch 3, bpdc around each of next 4 bpdc, *fpdc dec around next 2 sts, 2 bpdc around next bpdc, bpdc around each of next 3 bpdc, 2 bpdc around next bpdc, fpdc around each of next 3 sts, V-st in next ch-1 sp, fpdc around each of next 3 sts, 2 bpdc around next bpdc, bpdc around each of next 3 sts, 2 bpdc around next bpdc, fpdc dec around next 2 sts, bpdc around each of next 5 bpdc, fpdc around each of next 3 fpdc, V-st in next ch-1 sp, fpdc around each of next 3 fpdc**, bpdc around each of next 5 sts, rep from * around, ending last rep at **, join in 3rd ch of beg ch-3. (8 V-sts, 96 bpdc, 56 fpdc)

Rnd 18: Sl st around next bpdc, ch 3, *bpdc around next bpdc, bpdc dec around next 2 sts, fpdc around next fpdc, bpdc around each of next 7 bpdc, fpdc around each of next 4 fpdc, V-st in next ch-1 sp, fpdc around each of next 4 fpdc, bpdc around each of next 7 bpdc, fpdc around next fpdc, bpdc dec around next 2 sts, bpdc around next bpdc, bpdc dec around next 2 sts, fpdc around each of next 4 fpdc, V-st in next ch-1 sp, fpdc around each of next 4 fpdc**, bpdc dec around next 2 sts, rep from * around, ending last rep at **, join in 3rd ch of beg ch-3. (4 V-sts, 80 bpdc, 72 fpdc)

Rnd 19: Ch 3, bpdc around each of next 2 bpdc, *fpdc around next fpdc, bpdc dec around next 2 sts, bpdc around each of next 3 bpdc, bpdc dec around next 2 sts, fpdc around each of next 5 fpdc, V-st in next ch-1 sp, fpdc around each of next 5 fpdc, bpdc dec around next 2 sts, bpdc around each of next

3 bpdc, bpdc dec around next 2 sts, fpdc around next fpdc, bpdc around each of next 3 bpdc, fpdc around each of next 5 fpdc, V-st in next ch-1 sp, fpdc around each of next 5 fpdc**, bpdc around each of next 3 bpdc, rep from * around, ending last rep at **, join in 3rd ch of beg ch-3. Fasten off. (8 V-sts, 64 bpdc, 88 fpdc)

Side Band

Note: *Side Bands in sc are joined to Motifs and create depth of Handbag. If desired, skip instructions and join Motifs with slip stitches. However, Handbag will be flatter and not have the same depth as shown.*

First Band

Row 1: Ch 132, sc in 2nd ch from hook and in each rem ch across, turn. (131 sc)

Rows 2–10: Ch 1, sc in each sc across, turn. Do not fasten off.

Joining Side Band to Handbag

Getting started: Hold 1 Motif with RS facing, beg from first st on last rnd and counting clockwise, mark 72nd st (see Photo A).

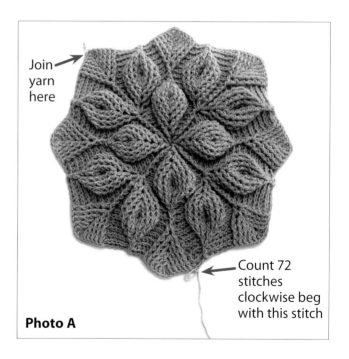

Join yarn here

Count 72 stitches clockwise beg with this stitch

Photo A

Joining row: Hold first st of large edge of First Band behind marked st, ch 1, sl st in marked st and corresponding st on First Band, working through both thicknesses at same time, sl st in each of next 130 sts *(see Photo B)*. Fasten off.

Photo B

2nd Band
Work same as First Band joining to Motifs in same manner.

Edging
Join yarn in any st at top edge of Handbag, ch 1, sc in each st around, join in first sc. Fasten off.

Handle
Make 2.

Row 1: With H hook, ch 141, sc in 2nd ch from hook and in each rem ch across, turn. *(140 sc)*

Rows 2–6: Ch 1, sc in each sc across, turn.

Fold piece so first row is aligned to last row. Working through sts on both rows, ch 1, sl st in first st and in each of next 139 sts *(see Photo C)*, roll end of Handle up 8 inches and tack roll section with a few sewn stitches made with yarn needle and yarn *(see Photo D)*.

Photo C

Finishing
Sew large toggle button on center point at top. Use ch-1 sp on opposite side as a buttonhole. ●

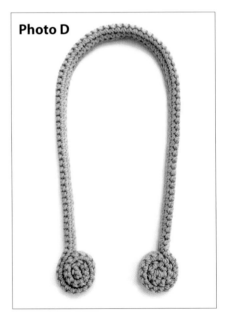

Photo D

STITCH GUIDE

Need help? ▶ **StitchGuide.com** • ILLUSTRATED GUIDES • HOW-TO VIDEOS

STITCH ABBREVIATIONS

beg	begin/begins/beginning
bpdc	back post double crochet
bpsc	back post single crochet
bptr	back post treble crochet
CC	contrasting color
ch(s)	chain(s)
ch-	refers to chain or space previously made (i.e., ch-1 space)
ch sp(s)	chain space(s)
cl(s)	cluster(s)
cm	centimeter(s)
dc	double crochet (singular/plural)
dc dec	double crochet 2 or more stitches together, as indicated
dec	decrease/decreases/decreasing
dtr	double treble crochet
ext	extended
fpdc	front post double crochet
fpsc	front post single crochet
fptr	front post treble crochet
g	gram(s)
hdc	half double crochet
hdc dec	half double crochet 2 or more stitches together, as indicated
inc	increase/increases/increasing
lp(s)	loop(s)
MC	main color
mm	millimeter(s)
oz	ounce(s)
pc	popcorn(s)
rem	remain/remains/remaining
rep(s)	repeat(s)
rnd(s)	round(s)
RS	right side
sc	single crochet (singular/plural)
sc dec	single crochet 2 or more stitches together, as indicated
sk	skip/skipped/skipping
sl st(s)	slip stitch(es)
sp(s)	space(s)/spaced
st(s)	stitch(es)
tog	together
tr	treble crochet
trtr	triple treble crochet
WS	wrong side
yd(s)	yard(s)
yo	yarn over

YARN CONVERSION

OUNCES TO GRAMS		GRAMS TO OUNCES	
1	28.4	25	⅞
2	56.7	40	1⅔
3	85.0	50	1¾
4	113.4	100	3½

UNITED STATES		UNITED KINGDOM
sl st (slip stitch)	=	sc (single crochet)
sc (single crochet)	=	dc (double crochet)
hdc (half double crochet)	=	htr (half treble crochet)
dc (double crochet)	=	tr (treble crochet)
tr (treble crochet)	=	dtr (double treble crochet)
dtr (double treble crochet)	=	ttr (triple treble crochet)
skip	=	miss

Single crochet decrease (sc dec): (Insert hook, yo, draw lp through) in each of the sts indicated, yo, draw through all lps on hook.

Example of 2-sc dec

Half double crochet decrease (hdc dec): (Yo, insert hook, yo, draw lp through) in each of the sts indicated, yo, draw through all lps on hook.

Example of 2-hdc dec

Reverse single crochet (reverse sc): Ch 1, sk first st, working from left to right, insert hook in next st from front to back, draw up lp on hook, yo and draw through both lps on hook.

Chain (ch): Yo, pull through lp on hook.

Single crochet (sc): Insert hook in st, yo, pull through st, yo, pull through both lps on hook.

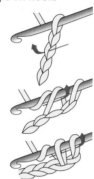

Double crochet (dc): Yo, insert hook in st, yo, pull through st, [yo, pull through 2 lps] twice.

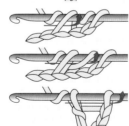

Double crochet decrease (dc dec): (Yo, insert hook, yo, draw lp through, yo, draw through 2 lps on hook) in each of the sts indicated, yo, draw through all lps on hook.

Example of 2-dc dec

Front loop (front lp) Back loop (back lp)

Front Loop   Back Loop

Front post stitch (fp): Back post stitch (bp): When working post st, insert hook from right to left around post of st on previous row.

Back   Front

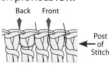

Post of Stitch

Half double crochet (hdc): Yo, insert hook in st, yo, pull through st, yo, pull through all 3 lps on hook.

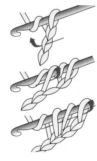

Double treble crochet (dtr): Yo 3 times, insert hook in st, yo, pull through st, [yo, pull through 2 lps] 4 times.

Treble crochet decrease (tr dec): Holding back last lp of each st, tr in each of the sts indicated, yo, pull through all lps on hook.

Example of 2-tr dec

Slip stitch (sl st): Insert hook in st, pull through both lps on hook.

Chain color change (ch color change) Yo with new color, draw through last lp on hook.

Double crochet color change (dc color change) Drop first color, yo with new color, draw through last 2 lps of st.

Treble crochet (tr): Yo twice, insert hook in st, yo, pull through st, [yo, pull through 2 lps] 3 times.

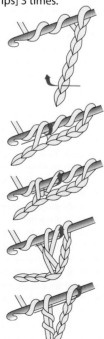

Metric Conversion Charts

METRIC CONVERSIONS

yards	x	.9144	=	metres (m)
yards	x	91.44	=	centimetres (cm)
inches	x	2.54	=	centimetres (cm)
inches	x	25.40	=	millimetres (mm)
inches	x	.0254	=	metres (m)

centimetres	x	.3937	=	inches
metres	x	1.0936	–	yards

INCHES INTO MILLIMETRES & CENTIMETRES (Rounded off slightly)

inches	mm	cm	inches	cm	inches	cm	inches	cm
1/8	3	0.3	5	12.5	21	53.5	38	96.5
1/4	6	0.6	5 1/2	14	22	56	39	99
3/8	10	1	6	15	23	58.5	40	101.5
1/2	13	1.3	7	18	24	61	41	104
5/8	15	1.5	8	20.5	25	63.5	42	106.5
3/4	20	2	9	23	26	66	43	109
7/8	22	2.2	10	25.5	27	68.5	44	112
1	25	2.5	11	28	28	71	45	114.5
1 1/4	32	3.2	12	30.5	29	73.5	46	117
1 1/2	38	3.8	13	33	30	76	47	119.5
1 3/4	45	4.5	14	35.5	31	79	48	122
2	50	5	15	38	32	81.5	49	124.5
2 1/2	65	6.5	16	40.5	33	84	50	127
3	75	7.5	17	43	34	86.5		
3 1/2	90	9	18	46	35	89		
4	100	10	19	48.5	36	91.5		
4 1/2	115	11.5	20	51	37	94		

KNITTING NEEDLES CONVERSION CHART

Canada/U.S.	0	1	2	3	4	5	6	7	8	9	10	10½	11	13	15
Metric (mm)	2	2¼	2¾	3¼	3½	3¾	4	4½	5	5½	6	6½	8	9	10

CROCHET HOOKS CONVERSION CHART

Canada/U.S.	1/B	2/C	3/D	4/E	5/F	6/G	8/H	9/I	10/J	10½/K	N
Metric (mm)	2.25	2.75	3.25	3.5	3.75	4.25	5	5.5	6	6.5	9.0

Annie's® *Learn Embossed Crochet* is published by Annie's, 306 East Parr Road, Berne, IN 46711. Printed in USA. Copyright © 2017 Annie's. All rights reserved. This publication may not be reproduced in part or in whole without written permission from the publisher.

RETAIL STORES: If you would like to carry this publication or any other Annie's publication, visit AnniesWSL.com.

Every effort has been made to ensure that the instructions in this publication are complete and accurate. We cannot, however, take responsibility for human error, typographical mistakes or variations in individual work. Please visit AnniesCustomerService.com to check for pattern updates.

ISBN: 978-1-57367-610-6

1 2 3 4 5 6 7 8 9